REDEFINING ENTREPRENEURIAL SUCCESS

A GUIDE TO A HEALTHY AND HOLISTIC LIFESTYLE

MARIA L. ELLIS, MBA

Difference Press

Washington, DC, USA

Published 2021

DISCLAIMER

Cover Design: Jennifer Stimson

Editing: Cory Hott

"Maria Ellis has defined what it means to live successfully as an entrepreneur versus just being a successful businessperson. As a former work-a-holic, I really appreciate her insights and wisdom. I wish someone had given me these insights thirty-five years ago when I started my first business. It took years to realize what is truly important. Maria has hit the nail on the head. A must read for all no matter where you are in your career."

— MAGGIE ROTH, PUBLISHED AUTHOR
AND CEO OF INVESTING BUDDIES, INC.

"I highly recommend reading and applying the concepts introduced by *Redefining Entrepreneurial Success: A Guide to a Healthy and Holistic Lifestyle*. Maria Ellis' poignant examples and stories lend further credence to the practical tips and tools that are relevant across cultures. She effortlessly captures the unique, and sometimes difficult to articulate, aspects of people's physical, emotional, and spiritual needs. Her book is a must-read for all entrepreneurs who are first or multiple generation family business owners grappling with balancing self-care and building a business."

— DR. BENJAMIN HARDY, PUBLISHED AUTHOR AND ORGANIZATIONAL PSYCHOLOGIST

"*Redefining Entrepreneurial Success: A Guide to a Healthy and Holistic Lifestyle* is a must-read for all entrepreneurs who are trying to balance self-care and building a business. Maria Ellis' examples and stories lend further credence to the practical tips and tools that are relevant across cultures. She effortlessly captures the unique aspects of people's physical, emotional, and spiritual needs."

— MARTA PANERO, PHD, EXECUTIVE
DIRECTOR AT NEW YORK INSTITUTE OF
TECHNOLOGY, STRATEGIC
COMMUNICATIONS AND EXTERNAL
AFFAIRS

"Maria Ellis shows us that health is a state of physical, emotional, mental and spiritual wellbeing and that to be successful throughout your life you need to maintain, and ideally strengthen, your health in all these dimensions. Her book lays out a comprehensive, varied set of easy-to-use techniques, behaviours and routines which will allow you to improve your health in all these dimensions. You will lead a healthier, happier and more successful live if you employ lessons from this book. Immensely insightful and beneficial."

— PETER SEWING OBERMARK, GMBH

"In her latest book, Maria Ellis, MBA, offers valuable insights into the health benefits of self-care. For many business owners who have heard about having morning and evening routines but remain reluctant to try them, Maria offers an accessible, easy, and enjoyable process that is centered not on the idea of lack of time but on committing and thriving on a healthy and holistic lifestyle."

— BRANDON STEINER,
COLLECTIBLEXCHANGE

"In this timely, interdisciplinary look at self-care as a practical ritual, Maria Ellis advances a powerful new paradigm for accomplishing more with daily morning and evening routines. *Redefining Entrepreneurial Success: A Guide to a Healthy and Holistic Lifestyle* is a timeless manifesto of mental, emotional, physical, and spiritual rewards of self-care and inner wisdom."

— TIMOTHY PAULSON, GENIUS NETWORK

CONTENTS

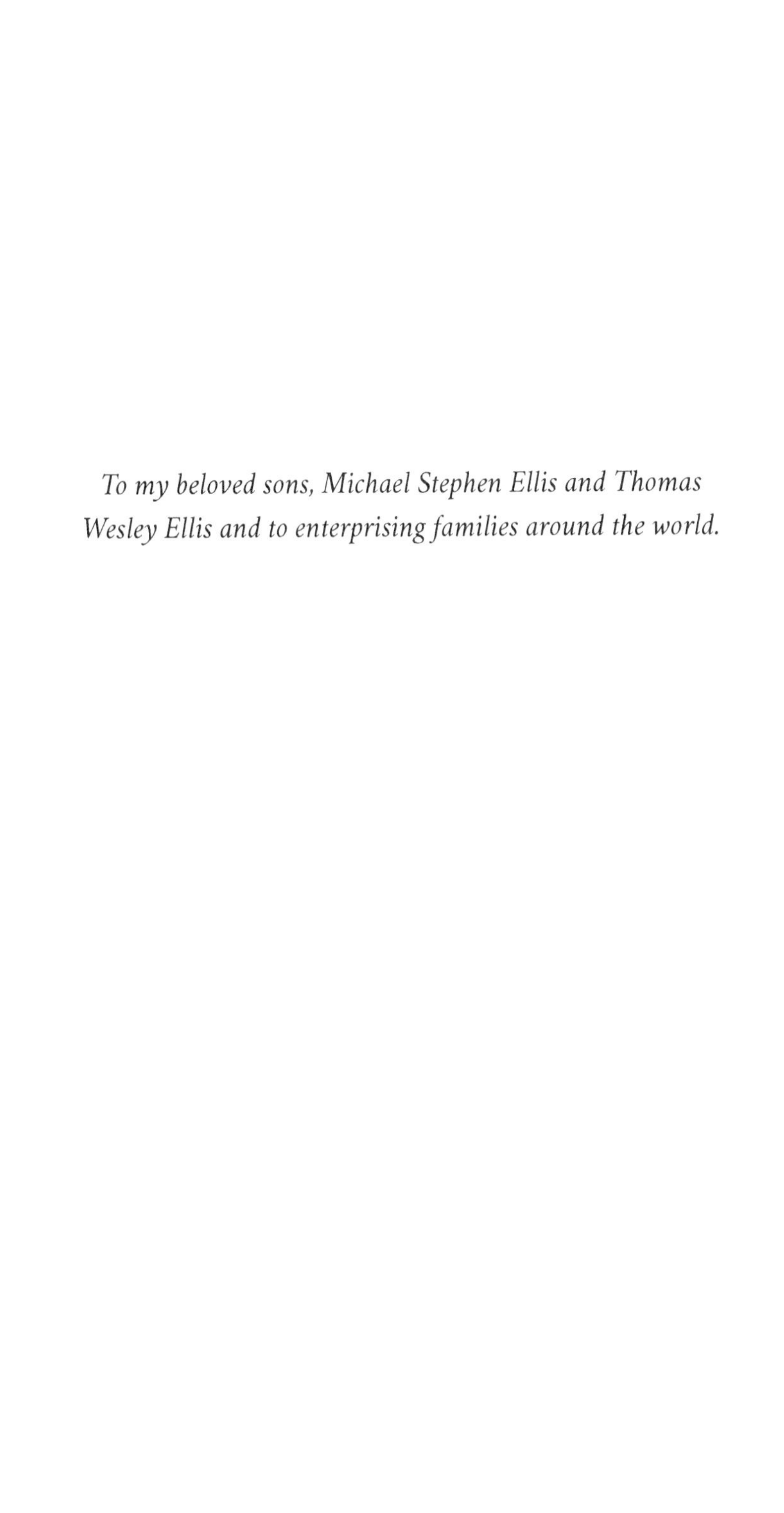

To my beloved sons, Michael Stephen Ellis and Thomas Wesley Ellis and to enterprising families around the world.

Maria L. Ellis has written a practical guide to a healthy and holistic lifestyle for busy entrepreneurs. Her book, *Redefining Entrepreneurial Success: A Guide to a Healthy and Holistic Lifestyle*, is about a topic that is always important, generation after generation: how to ensure that entrepreneurs build successful businesses and enjoy a good health and longevity. As a Chopra Certified Health Instructor, Maria captures both the mind and the heart of self-care and does so in a fluid and accessible manner. Her poignant examples and stories lend further credence to the practical tips and tools that are relevant across cultures. She effortlessly captures the unique, and sometimes difficult to articulate, aspects of living a healthy and holistic lifestyle through self-care.

Maria's life story is inspiring. Immigrating to the

United States with her family after graduating from high school in Guayaquil, Ecuador where she was born and spent her formative years, Maria pursued her BBA and MBA at the University of Massachusetts, and later enrolled in the Harvard Business School Owner-President Management program. This education allowed Maria to pursue her professional dreams and is a great example of the pillars in successful personal financial management which are: saving, investing, and estate planning.

Maria's analysis goes beyond simple self-care. This is not simply a to do list, but a holistic strategic approach to maintaining good health and longevity. This book builds on the foundational tools of Maria's best-selling books, *Achieve Financial Freedom* and *Family Business Legacy Plan*, which serve as a helpful reference guide as you reach each of your personal and personal financial milestones. I should add that Maria possesses a great work ethic: she commits to doing her best in all that she takes on. In addition to her advisory services, Maria is a pro-bono consultant with the Harvard Business School Club of New York's Community Partners whose mission is to create constructive partnerships between Harvard Business School alumni and nonprofit organizations in the greater New York City metropolitan area that seek assistance with business and management issues.

Like Maria, I am a graduate of the Owner-President Management Program at Harvard Business

School, and I know that a healthy lifestyle, a positive outlook in life, and a grateful heart are the keys to success. These are the important values that I have learned and will be nurturing after I read Maria Ellis's book, *Redefining Entrepreneurial Success: A Guide to a Healthy and Holistic Lifestyle*. I have also restructured my morning and evening rituals. I now start my morning rituals with a quick early morning meditation. Meditation is a simple practice available to all, which can reduce stress, increase calmness and clarity, and promote happiness. Learning how to meditate is straightforward, and the benefits can come quickly. In Ellis's book, it offers basic tips to get you started on a path toward greater equanimity, acceptance, and joy. Take a deep breath and get ready to relax though the journey of mindfulness to success.

Mental health is one of the greatest challenges of most CEO's specially this pandemic. Most leaders and entrepreneurs are facing the fact that all businesses have to re-pivot, restructure and refocus their goals and targets in this pandemic. Key result areas, key performance indicators, and scorecards must be redefined, hence, it causes a lot of stress to most entrepreneurs. This book allows you to find your inner core and balance things in perspective (especially the language of laughter), I highly recommend this book and will live by what it shares. It will make every entrepreneur conquer and soar greater heights with Ellis's insights. Congratulations,

Maria Ellis! A job well done, and it will be the new bible for entrepreneurs to lead a happy, healthy, and balanced life.

> — PINKY TOBIANO, FOUNDER AND CEO
> QUALIBET TESTING SERVICES

MY HIGH STRESS LEVEL AND UNHEALTHY LIFESTYLE ARE DETRIMENTAL TO MY HEALTH AND WELLBEING

"Take care of your body. It's the only place you have to live."

— JIM ROHN

I was talking with one of my dearest clients, an entrepreneur named Michael, about the idea of writing this book to teach business owners about the importance of self-care. Michael spends enormous amounts of time and energy on his business, which he wants to take to the next level of performance and profitability. I emphasized how entrepreneurs need to take care of their bodies, minds, and spirits to obtain the clarity required to achieve such success. Michael immediately replied, "My day is full. I have no time for such wellness activities." He further said, "I will do wellness *after* I build a high-performance culture that results in business success." Michael proceeded to ask, "Did Steve Jobs or does Elon Musk practice such things? If not, I am not interested."

As proven by Steve Jobs and Elon Musk, entrepreneurial work is an all-consuming focus for business owners. We all know that Steve Jobs was known to be an extreme workaholic with some peculiar health habits, which reportedly included extreme fasting and even all-fruit and carrots diets. Fruits and fruit juices are not only high on the glycemic index but are also loaded with fructose. In all but small quantities, they greatly stress the liver and pancreas, contribute to diabetes and many other blood sugar disorders, and increase the risk of pancreatic cancer. Jobs suffered from a type of pancreatic cancer known as islet cell carcinoma, which originates in the insulin-secreting beta cells.

While some of Elon Musk's pursuits in brain health and technology may seem surreal, his health and fitness habits are relatable. "The older I get, the harder it is to stay lean. That's for sure," the Tesla CEO said on a recent episode of The Joe Rogan Experience podcast. In the interview, the forty-nine-year-old billionaire added that he likes eating "tasty food" and wishes he could do without exercise. Here is what else Musk said he does: "To be totally frank, I wouldn't exercise at all if I could," Musk said. "I prefer not to exercise. Instead, I prefer to lift some weights." Musk's unconventional approach to food also raised eyebrows in the past. "If there was a way that I could not eat so I could work more, I would not eat," he was quoted as saying in the 2015 book Elon Musk: Tesla, SpaceX, and the Quest for a Fantastic Future by Ashlee Vance.

My client Michael recognizes and acknowledges that Fortune 500 companies have wellness programs for their teams. Research shows that more companies prioritize employee mental health initiatives now. From training managers about how to spot mental health issues among team members – and what to do if they suspect them – to providing support for employees who are struggling, there is an increased awareness about providing resources and developing and training managers on how to talk about them. Michael comments that "large Fortune 500 companies can afford such wellness programs, but the small- to medium-size business owners do not have the time and cannot afford such luxury." My response is that especially the small and medium-size entrepreneurs cannot afford not to have a wellness program for them and for their employees.

According to the Harvard Business Review, more employees are working when they are sick, costing employers about $150 billion to $250 billion or 60 percent of the total cost of worker illness. Additionally, chronic diseases; a rapidly aging workforce; and factors like stress, fatigue, and depression all affect employers' revenue. The Center for Disease Control and Prevention (CDC) reports that productivity losses linked to absenteeism cost employers $225.8 billion annually in the United States, or $1,685 per employee. Promoting safe and healthy work practices boosts profitability and productivity among employers of all sizes. Business Pulse: Healthy Workforce, launched by the CDC Foundation, provides employers and workers with access to resources and information to help improve workforce health and safety and attract and retain high-performing employees and minimize healthcare costs.

The CDC plays a critical role in helping the U.S. businesses remain competitive and productive through guidance to encourage safer, healthier workplaces. Business Pulse: Healthy Workforce provides information and practical tools from the CDC to help employers prevent injuries and illnesses and promote employees' health and well-being. "The health and safety of the American workforce is vital to the U.S. economy," said L. Casey Chosewood, MD, MPH, director of the Office for Total Worker Health at the National Institute for Occupational Safety and Health at CDC. "CDC plays a critical role in helping U.S. businesses remain competitive and productive through guidance to encourage safer, healthier workplaces."

Business Pulse highlights specific workforce health challenges faced by businesses as well as a question-and-answer feature between a CDC workforce health expert and a mid-sized employer, Lincoln Industries. Employers learn about CDC programs that aim to create organizational cultures of health and safety and gain valuable tools, guidelines, and resources through an interactive infographic. Business Pulse: Healthy Workforce is the sixth in a series of quarterly business features created by the CDC Foundation, an independent nonprofit organization. Other Business Pulse topics to date include business continuity, safe healthcare, global health security, travelers' health, and flu prevention.

As a Chopra Certified Health Instructor and Practitioner, it is my duty and my pleasure to introduce you to the Ayurvedic lifestyle. Dissecting the word "Ayurveda," "Ayur" means "life," and "veda" means "science" or "knowledge." Ayurveda is a 5,000-year-old consciousness-based system of healing from India. Its purpose is to help us return to our natural state of health, balance, and wholeness. Ayurveda recognizes the primacy of consciousness and offers powerful practices that can help us change the qualities of our experiences in consciousness to create health and balance in our mind-body system. Our essential and ground state is pure consciousness, pure potentiality, and the field of all possibilities. Consciousness is the source of all our experiences, including our sensations, images, feelings, thoughts, imagination, creativity, perceptions, insight, and intuition.

Ayurvedic practices include sensory modulation, meditation, yoga, nutrition, emotional wellbeing, physical activity, breathing practices, daily routines, and many other tools and practices for shifting our consciousness toward health and happiness. Ayurveda is experiential, and there is no one-size-fits-all prescription for wellbeing. Instead, every health-related measure is based on an individual's mind-body type, or dosha, and the needs that derive from it. The six most important pillars of health to focus on in a daily lifestyle are sleep, meditation, movement/ physical activity, healthy emotions, self-care, and optimal nutrition.

The five building blocks of nature that make up everything we perceive through our senses are air, space, water, fire, and earth. These exist both within us and in the world around us. Begin thinking of yourself as a multidimensional being. Notice how your awareness expands or constricts. Become familiar with your energy (dosha) qualities and characteristics to bring awareness and notice when imbalances arise. Take steps to restore balance. Remember, there is no one-size-fits-all prescription for wellbeing.

Current scientific research validates Ayurvedic techniques. Ayurvedic techniques can change gene expression to promote healing, self-regulation, and homeostasis (balance). Studies conducted at the Chopra Center's Perfect Health program and the Seduction of Spirit programs reported that the participants experienced reductions in anxiety, sustained increases in psychological wellbeing, and decreases in chemicals that may reduce the risk of heart disease.

In summary, your body and mind are dynamic and constantly transforming. You are not a static, physical machine that learned manufactured thoughts, emotions, and ideas. Rather, you are a network of intelligence in dynamic exchange with everything that surrounds you. Therefore, no matter how busy you are running your company, you must also make time to take care of your body, mind, and soul. They are inseparable parts of the infinite field of intelligence. The physical world, including your body, reflects your perceptions, thoughts, and feelings.

2

I SOLVED MY STRESSFUL LIFE BY CREATING HEALTHY MORNING AND EVENING ROUTINES

"To keep the body in good health is a duty, otherwise we shall not be able to keep our mind strong and clear."

— BUDDHA

I, too, used to think that I did not have time for such wellness activities and that I would create and implement a wellness program after my company was profitable. I was running a financial services company, my husband was an entrepreneur, and we were raising two boys. I was busy taking care of my family, my clients, and everyone else who needed my help. I was so busy and tired that I did not pay attention to my health. Suddenly, one early morning, I woke up with such an intense pain that I could not get up from my bed. I tried many times to get up from bed to clean up a bit, but the pain was so severe that all I could say to my husband was, "Please take me to the hospital."

When the doctors examined me, they recommended I get an operation immediately. Being a busy entrepreneur, I did not maintain a healthy eating or exercise schedule. I told myself I did not have time for self-care. After having to have my gallbladder removed, I realized that I had been eating the wrong foods: fatty foods, fried foods, dairy products, sugary foods, and carbonated soft drinks, which triggered my gallbladder attacks. I had been so busy taking care of everyone else that I did not seek medical attention until the situation was so dire that I had to seek medical treatment. This behavior is typical of many entrepreneurs.

After I had my gallbladder removed, I paid closer attention to my health, ate better, and exercised daily. I found karate and yoga to be most enjoyable. I like karate because my two sons, Michael and Tommy, and my husband, Stephen, took karate at the YMCA.

Karate offers a way to relax; it's a moving meditation. Some of the benefits of Karate include increased confidence, flexibility, better coordination, and knowledge of self-defense skills. Also, karate lowers blood pressure and heart rate. Recent research shows that aerobic exercise, like martial arts, produces a physical change in the brain that promotes better memory and learning skills. We enjoyed taking karate lessons as a family because it was a team environment. I was working alongside people with the same goals and learning and growing together. We also improved our social skills in addition to teaching self-discipline for our young boys and teaching ourselves self-reliance and independence. My husband and my two boys obtained their black belts in karate. It was a fun family experience for over a decade.

Although I enjoyed karate, my favorite exercise was yoga because it boosted my energy, increased my flexibility, and improved my posture and appearance. Most postures require the center to be locked in and the shoulders pulled back. Unlike karate, which is a team activity, yoga is an internal and individual practice. The attention is on what's going on inside you. Yoga helped me with my sleep apnea. The signs and symptoms of obstructive and central sleep apneas overlap, sometimes making it difficult to determine which type you have. The most common signs and symptoms of obstructive and central sleep apneas include loud snoring, episodes in which you stop breathing during sleep, gasps for air during sleep, a dry mouth upon awakening, difficulty staying asleep (insomnia), excessive daytime sleepiness (hypersomnia), difficulty paying attention while awake, and irritability. It was also around this time, when I was raising my two sons, that my mother Jenny passed away at a relatively young age. It was a huge loss for me, and the pain was so deep that

I was only able to accept the loss and release the sadness and pain by doing the deep breathing and inner work.

It was not until I became a Chopra Certified Health Instructor that I created morning and evening self-care routines that included pranayama to enable me to solve my stressful life by minimizing my stress and enjoying a healthy lifestyle. Pranayama is the practice of becoming aware of your breath and using it to enhance your physical, emotional, and spiritual well-being. "Prana" means "vital life force," and "ayama" means to expand, draw out, and control. Pranayama enables you to use the breath to expand life force energy and improve communication among all parts of the body-mind system. Our breathing influences our thoughts and physiology. When the mind is calm, breathing is deep and rhythmic, and the body engages in its natural self-repairing, self-healing mechanisms.

In summary, I will teach business owners my optimal morning and evening routine, which includes waking up early in the morning, approximately 6:00 a.m.; performing yoga, flexibility exercises, and mindful movements; meditating; and practicing pranayama. My clients will learn how to create an optimal evening routine, including eating a light dinner around 6:00 p.m. and walking for five to fifteen minutes to aid digestion. My clients will perform light activity in the evening, such as getting their schedule ready for the next day, minimizing intense mental work and electronic stimulation, and aiming to be in bed with the lights off by 10:30 p.m. In this book, I will teach you the concepts, techniques, and practices that I use to keep my mind, body, and spirit healthy so I can run my businesses effectively and profitably.

3

HOW BEST TO CREATE A HEALTHY AND HARMONIOUS LIFESTYLE?

"The greatest wealth is health."

— VIRGIL

In this chapter, I will teach you how to create a healthy and harmonious lifestyle. To create a healthy daily routine, you need to align yourself with nature's rhythms to facilitate the body's natural processes of digestion, detoxification, healing, maximize health and longevity with periods of activity, including mindful movement, and periods of rest, including a healthy sleep routine. Nature moves and flows in patterns of rest and activity. The rhythms of nature are the circadian, the twenty-four-hour cycle of night and day; seasonal, the twelve-month cycle of the Earth around the Sun; lunar, the monthly cycle of the Moon around the Earth; and Tidal, the gravitational influence of the moon on water. The circadian rhythm is a twenty-four-hour cycle of night and day.

You have doshas, or bio-energy centers, derived from the five natural elements: air, space, water, fire, and earth. A combination of each element results in three doshas. In Ayurvedic medicine, each of the three energies (Vata, Pitta, and Kapha) circulate in the body and govern our physiological activity. The best hours for the Vata dosha are from 2:00 a.m. to 6:00 a.m. and from 2:00 p.m. to 6:00 p.m. The Vata dosha is creative, productive, and high energy. The best hours for Kapha dosha are from 6:00 a.m. to 10:00 a.m. and from 6:00 p.m. to 10:00 p.m. The Kapha dosha benefits from a daily exercise routine early in the morning. The best hours for the Pitta dosha are from 10:00 a.m. to 2:00 p.m. and from 10:00 p.m. to 2:00 a.m. A Pitta dosha has a strong Agni and enjoys deep sleep. Click on the link below for a fun video on lifestyle(s) based on your own dosha(s): bit.ly/3pdA7jF.

The Ayurvedic concept of fire, or agni, is critically important to our overall health. Agni is the force of intelligence within each cell, each tissue, and every system within the body. If you do not know your dosha (mind-body type), click on the following link, take the quiz and enjoy: https://chopra.com/dosha-quiz.

THE SEASONAL CYCLES

Seasonal influences may affect your level of balance.

Vata Season: Late fall through winter. Vata balancing techniques counter the effects of seasonal influences. Vata doshas favor warm food and drinks and sweet, sour, and salty tastes. Vata doshas need to reduce pungent, bitter, and astringent tastes and dry and raw foods. They need to stay warm, grounded, and hydrated.

Kapha Season: Late winter through spring. Kapha balancing techniques to counter the effects of seasonal influences. Kapha doshas favor a lighter diet, warm foods, and drinks. They need to eat more pungent, bitter, astringent tastes and dress to stay warm and enjoy daily enlivening exercises.

Pitta Season: Summer through early fall. Pitta balancing techniques counter the effects of seasonal influences. Pitta doshas favor cooling foods and drinks of sweet, bitter, and astringent tastes. Need to reduce sour, salty, and pungent tastes. Avoid overheating when exercising. Use cooling aromas.

Times of Change: During times of season changes, it is best to simplify your diet during times of transformation. Occasional fasting can be a useful tool. Nourish yourself and cultivate peace and clarity by releasing negative emotions. Journaling is highly recommended.

Enhancing Life Force: Here are a few ways to

enhance your life force: Gaze into the night sky (Space); walk in abundant vegetation, ideally at dusk and dawn (Air); allow the light and warmth of the sun to permeate you (Fire); walk along with natural bodies of water (Water); walk barefoot on natural earth (Earth); and do Pranayama practices.

Mindful Movement: Exercise for balancing the three doshas: Essential components of a complete fitness program are flexibility, strength, and cardio.

- Vata Balancing: Tai chi, yoga, walking, short hikes, light bicycling.
- Pitta Balancing: Brisk walking or jogging, swimming, biking, snowboarding, skiing, and outdoor activities. Avoid overheating and avoid being overly competitive
- Kapha Balancing: Enjoy vigorous and longer workouts and movements, running, cardio, dance, rowing, active yoga, and weight training.

As you practice the Ayurvedic lifestyle, observe how these daily practices help you cultivate a lifestyle to support your physical, emotional, and spiritual wellbeing. Integrate the optimal daily routines. Stay in harmony with the changing seasons.

As a Kapha, here is my optimal morning routine.

- Awaken without an alarm clock at approximately 6:00 a.m.
- Drink a glass of warm water.
- Empty bowels/ bladder.
- Brush teeth/ clean tongue
- Oil pulling, an alternative mouthwash practice. Oil pulling is an alternative medical practice in which an edible oil is swished around the mouth and then spat out.
- Cleanse nasal passage with neti and nasya.
- Perform flexibility exercises/mindful movements/ yoga.
- Meditate and practice pranayama.
- Oil massage/ bathe.
- Eat a nutritious breakfast with awareness.
- Perform morning work/ activities.

As a Kapha, here is my optimal noon routine.

- Eat lunch (largest meal of the day): 12:00 p.m. to 1:00 p.m.
- Sit quietly for five minutes after eating.
- Walk for five to fifteen minutes to aid digestion.
- Perform afternoon work/ activity.
- Meditation and pranayama in the late afternoon

As a Kapha, here is my optimal evening routine.

- Eat a light dinner at least two hours before bedtime.
- Sit quietly for five minutes after eating.
- Walk for five to fifteen minutes to aid digestion.
- Enjoy light activity in the evening.
- Minimize intense mental work and electronic stimulation.
- Aim to be in bed with the lights off by 10:30 p.m.

MY RESTFUL SLEEP

As a Kapha, I aim for a 10:30 p.m. bedtime with all lights and electronics off, practice calming pranayama and gentle yoga, have a soothing self-massage and a warm bath with lavender, and avoid caffeine late in the day and alcohol in the evening. I enjoy drinking herbal teas, such as chamomile, and reading inspirational/ spiritual literature. I also enjoy journaling to download my thoughts and the events of the day. I write down what I am grateful for daily, which is a form of recapitulation. I read inspirational or spiritual literature. Once in bed, I close my eyes, tune into my body and breath, and easily fall asleep. The quality of our sensory impressions (ears, skin, eyes, tongue, and nose) determines our thoughts and feelings. The ears, skin, eyes, tongue, and nose are the gateways through which we experience the world. To balance the mind, focus on the sense of sound, smell, and sight. To balance the body, focus on taste and touch. The doshas are tuned into nature: Vata relates to sound and touch; Pitta to sight; and Kapha to taste and smell.

BALANCING YOUR DOSHAS THROUGH SOUND

Sound can create harmony within your mind, body, emotions, and spirit. Sounds of nature have vibrational qualities. Mantras have specific meanings and purpose. Music is invigorating, calming, and soothing. The chakra sounds are awakening practices, and speech enables conscious communication. Click on the link below for an Inner Pharmacy video about balancing out doshas through sound: bit.ly/3mXLWaQ

BALANCING OUR DOSHAS THROUGH TOUCH

Regular massage and loving touch detoxify the body's tissues. A daily self-massage is an important aspect of daily routine because it calms the mind, improves circulation, and enhances immune function. Nourish your body with oils to balance your dosha. Vata likes heavier, warming oils, such as sesame or almond oil; Pitta enjoys cooling, soothing oils, such as coconut, sunflower, or olive oil; and Kapha favors light, warming oils, such as sunflower, safflower, or mustard oil.

BALANCING OUR DOSHAS THROUGH SIGHT

The images we ingest have a profound effect on our physiology, including our mind and emotions. Images and patterns can increase or decrease balance and harmony. Images of nature are calming and balancing. Violent images create imbalances. The balancing colors for each dosha are as follows: Vata likes earth tones and mild pastels; Pitta favors cool soft colors, such as light blues and greens; and Kapha prefers bright colors, like reds and oranges.

BALANCING OUR DOSHAS THROUGH TASTE

According to Dr. Deepak Chopra, Ayurveda believes the six tastes should be consumed every day to promote balance within the body. Vatas should focus on more sweet, salty, and sour tastes in their diets and limit pungent, bitter, and astringent tastes. Pittas need sweet, bitter, and astringent tastes more than pungent, sour, and salty tastes. Enjoy the colors of the rainbow and a wide variety of fresh, organic foods that support your Agni.

BALANCING OUR DOSHAS THROUGH SMELL

Aromas connect us to emotions, memory, and instincts. We can link a healing response to the experience of a particular smell. We can link a healing response to the experience of a particular smell. Use specific aromas for each dosha:

- Vata: Favors floral, fruity, warm, sweet, and sour, such as basil, orange, geranium, clove, vanilla, and patchouli.
- Pitta: Favors cooling and sweet, such as sandalwood, mint, rose, jasmine, and lavender.
- Kapha: Favors stimulating, spicy, and aromatic, such as eucalyptus, camphor, juniper, clove, and marjoram.

BALANCING OUR DOSHAS THROUGH LAUGHTER

Belly laughter enhances immune function. Laugh and enjoy the experiences of life. You can bring more laughter and joy into your life by setting the intent to laugh more. Make a resolution or set the intent of laughing heartily as often as you can. Setting a goal to laugh more is as important as setting the goals to get more exercise, eat healthier, and drink more water.

It is possible to become the person you want to

become and create the life you want. One of my clients, Stephanie was having a problem finding a way to balance her health with her work. I helped Stephanie to find inner peace by asking her, when she woke up in the morning, to – instead of rushing carelessly into her hectic day, feeling stressed and overwhelmed – instead spend the first few minutes sitting in purposeful silence, meditation, and reflection. Her morning routine included yoga, deep breathing, and saying a prayer of gratitude to appreciate the moment or praying for guidance on her daily activities.

You, too, may decide to try your first few minutes after waking up on reflection and meditation. As you sit in silence, you are totally present in the now. You can calm your mind, relax your body, and allow all your stress to melt away. You develop a deeper sense of peace, purpose, and direction.

I will help you create your own daily affirmations to remind you of your unlimited potential and your most important priorities. As you focus on what is most important to you, your level of internal motivation increases. Reading over the reminders of how capable you are gives you a feeling of confidence. Looking over what you are committed to, what your purpose is, and what your goals are re-energizes you to take the actions necessary to live the life you truly want, deserve, and know is possible for yourself.

During your morning routine, try closing your eyes or looking at your vision board and visualizing. Your visualization could include your goals and what it will look and feel like when you reach them. Visualize the day going perfectly. See yourself enjoying your work, smiling and laughing with your family or your significant other, and easily accomplishing all that you intend to accomplish for that day. You see what it will look like, you feel what it will feel like, and you experience the joy of what you will create daily. Also, I highly recommend that you take a few minutes to write down what you are grateful for, what you are proud of, and the results you are committed to creating for that day. By doing so, you put yourself in an empowered, inspired, and confident state of mind. I journal every day at the end of the day and enjoy all the serendipities and feel grateful for the many challenges and blessings that I experience each day.

One of my clients, Jackie, did not particularly like to read every day. As part of her daily evening routine, now she enjoys reading self-help books and invests a few minutes reading a page or two. You, too, can appreciate reading as a form of relaxation and learn a new idea and as something that you can implement into your day. You may discover something new that you can use to be and feel better.

There is a growing body of scientific research documenting the benefits of practicing pranayama on a regular basis, including reduced anxiety and depression, lower/ stabilized blood pressure, increased energy levels, relaxed muscles, and decreased feelings of stress and overwhelm. Mind-body interventions are beneficial in stress-related mental and physical disorders. Current research is finding associations between emotional disorders and vagal tone as indicated by heart rate variability. Wikipedia's definition of Vagal tone is the activity of the vagus nerve, the 10th cranial nerve and a fundamental component of the parasympathetic branch of the autonomic nervous system. This branch of the nervous system is not under conscious control and is largely responsible for the regulation of several body compartments at rest. Vagal activity results in various effects, including heart rate reduction, vasodilation/ constriction of vessels, glandular activity in the heart, lungs, and digestive tract, liver, and immune system.

Per the National Library of Medicine article written by Richard P Brown and Patricia L Gerbarg, a neurophysiologic model of yogic breathing proposes to integrate research on yoga with polyvagal theory, vagal stimulation, hyperventilation, and clinical observations. Polyvagal theory studies the body's neurological responses in relation to fear, stress, trauma, and anxiety in a new and groundbreaking way while being well researched and evidence based. Yogic breathing is a unique method for balancing the autonomic nervous system and influencing psychologic and stress-related disorders. Many studies demonstrate the effects of yogic breathing for brain function and physiologic parameters, but the mechanisms have not been clarified. Sudarshan Kriya yoga (SKY), a sequence of specific breathing techniques (ujjayi, bhastrika, and Sudarshan Kriya), can alleviate anxiety, depression, everyday stress, post-traumatic stress, and stress-related medical illnesses. Mechanisms contributing to a state of calm alertness include increased parasympathetic drive, calming of stress response systems, the neuroendocrine release of hormones, and thalamic generators.

Stress constantly creeps into our lives. It can come from the frustration of a traffic jam or a confrontation with a partner. Stress can be spurred by money worries or spiked by a sudden health scare. It can exact a toll upon you physically, emotionally, and psychologically. Stress is a fact of life. But you determine how it affects your life. You can counteract the damaging effects of stress by calling upon your body's rich potential for self-healing. Stress Management, a special health report from Harvard Medical School, is packed with strategies you can use to rein in the runaway changes unleashed by stress. To obtain a copy of this report, see the link below: https://www.coursehero.com/file/ 85419509/3-Strtess-Management-textbook-P52pdf/

Stress management will help you explore cognitive restructuring, a strategy to change the way you look at things. You will find how to challenge negative thoughts and avoid jumping to conclusions. And if you have heard about the power of visualization and meditation but don't know where to start, the report will show you. Learn how to identify the warning signs of stress. It will alert you to the dynamic roles of nutrition and social support. It will give you tips for coping with caregiver stress, work-related stress, and stress from conflict with others. And you will find three rewarding mental exercises that boost happiness. Learn to nurture yourself and use mindfulness to reduce workday stress. The Harvard Medical School issued a publication about how best to manage stress. For more details, click on the link below: My Book

Yoga breathing is an important part of health and spiritual practices in Indo-Tibetan traditions. Considered fundamental for the development of physical well-being, meditation, awareness, and enlightenment, it is both a form of meditation and preparation for deep meditation. Yoga breathing (pranayama) can rapidly bring the mind to the present moment and reduce stress. A yoga breathing, meditation, and longevity paper was published by the National Library of Medicine. It reviews data indicating how breathwork can affect longevity mechanisms in some ways that overlap with meditation and in other ways that are different from but synergistically enhance the effects of meditation. It also provides clinical evidence for the use of yoga breathing in the treatment of depression, anxiety, and post-traumatic stress disorder, and for victims of mass disasters. Click on the link below for more details: https://pubmed.ncbi.nlm.nih.gov/19735239/

Yoga has many health benefits. For example, coherent breathing is a form of breathing that involves taking long slow breaths at a rate of about five per minute. According to an article written by Arlin Cuncic and Sarah Clark, published in Verywell Mind, Coherent breathing or deep breathing, helps to calm the body through its effect on the autonomic nervous system. The health benefits of coherence breathing include decreased anxiety and depression, improved sleep, strengthened immune function, reduced inflammation, and increased resilience. To receive the full benefits, practice mindfully, then relax and sit quietly for a few moments before slowly resuming the activity. Sit comfortably on a chair or on the floor. Your eyes may be opened or closed. Place the hands on the belly if that feels comfortable. This will allow you to feel the belly move out on the inhale and in on the exhale. Relax the belly to let the breathing be effortless. Inhale, letting the belly expand into the hands for a count of four. Then, exhale, letting the belly gently draw into a count of five. Repeat this pattern and continue in this way for another three or four breaths.

Another yoga breathing method is the nadi (channel of circulation) shodhana (cleansing) method. This breathing method clears your emotional blockages and toxins, infuses the body-mind with energy and oxygen, harmonizes the brain's left and right hemispheres, reduces feelings of anxiety, and improves stress management and sleep. To receive the full benefits, practice for five to ten full rounds each day, consciously and mindfully, before each meditation and whenever you want to cultivate a sense of calm and balance. Sit comfortably with a straight spine with your left hand comfortably on your lap. Rest the tip of the index finger and middle finger of your right hand in between the eyebrows Close off the right nostril with the thumb. Inhale slowly through the left nostril to the top of the breath. Then, use the ring and pinky fingers to close off the left nostril. Release the thumb and slowly exhale through the right nostril to the bottom of the breath. Then, inhale through the right nostril to the top of the breath. Next, place the thumb back over the right nostril, and release the ring and pinky fingers to exhale through the left nostril to the bottom of the breath. Repeat this pattern for a few rounds.

My favorite yoga breathing is the ujjayi "victorious breath." Gentle and rhythmic breath produces a pleasant, soothing sound, like the sound of ocean waves, that calms and cools the mind, releases feelings of irritation or frustration, mildly warms and energizes the body from the core, and creates a stabilizing influence on the cardiorespiratory system. To receive the full benefits, practice for five to ten full rounds each day, gently, smoothly, and mindfully. Sit comfortably with a straight spine with your left hand comfortably on your lap. With the mouth gently closed, take an inhalation through the nose that is slightly deeper than normal.

Next, gently constrict the muscles at the back of the throat and exhale through the nose. This should produce a sound like the waves of the ocean. Keeping the throat muscles constricted, inhale again through the nose, and exhale through the nose. Repeat this pattern several times, gently and without straining. Another way to master this type of breath is to exhale the sound "haaaaaa" with the mouth open, as if trying to fog up a mirror. Now, make this same sound with the mouth closed, which will give the desired sound.

In summary, I have taught you how best to create a healthy and harmonious lifestyle by observing how your breathing is affected by your thoughts, and your thoughts and physiology are influenced by your breath. Live in gratitude for the primordial vital force that sustains you in every moment of your life.

4

NUTRITION

"Our food should be our medicine and our medicine should be our food."

— HIPPOCRATES

In this chapter, I will teach you some ideas about how to prepare balanced meals to increase your wellness with food that you enjoy. It is important to eat a variety of colorful foods to receive a broad spectrum of nutrients. The six basic nutrients in our meals are proteins, water, fats, carbohydrates, minerals, and vitamins. Proteins, carbohydrates, and fats provide energy. Proteins form important parts of the body's main structural components and have a major role in building and repairing. Carbohydrates are the body's preferred source of energy. Fats (lipids), in addition to providing the most concentrated form of energy, play a role in the storage and transportation of fat-soluble vitamins. Minerals and vitamins regulate body functions.

Deep pigments in plant foods are dense with nutrients and generally have more antioxidants. Cook with color to add visual appeal and encourage appreciation of a meal. Enhance your health with phytochemicals (plant chemicals) that have protective or disease-preventive properties. Some of the benefits include protection against oxidative damage and decreased risk of cancer and heart disease. The easiest way to get more phytochemicals is to eat more fruit and vegetables.

Ayurvedic lifestyle recommends eating your biggest meal in the middle of the day when your agni (digestive power) is the strongest. Avoid overeating and reduce ice-cold foods and beverages. It is also advisable to sit quietly for a few minutes after your meal while focusing attention on the body, then take a short walk to help digestion. What is agni? It is the metabolic power responsible for extracting nourishment and eliminating toxins. Your health depends on proper digestion. When our digestive fire is strong and healthy, we can easily digest food and experiences. We extract the greatest level of nourishment from our diet (ojas). Yogapedia's definition of "ojas" is "vigor." In the practice of Ayurveda, ojas is thought to be responsible for vitality, strength, health, long life, immunity, and mental/ emotional wellness. When our digestive fire is weak or irregular, we cannot properly digest even potentially nourishing substances, and our body starts to accumulate toxins (ama). We keep agni strong by eating the proper amount; eating the right foods; and managing stress, which can dampen agni.

What is microbiome? The microbiome is a vast colony of micro-organisms that inhabit our body, including bacteria and other microbes. These microbes live mainly in our digestive tract, in our mouth, and even on our skin. The microbiome is beneficial for our health; it helps to digest our food, regulate hormones and immune system, and influence our nervous system and emotions. In your daily life, the choices you make about what you eat can make the greatest difference in cultivating a healthy gut microbiome. You need to avoid refined and processed foods and favor fresh, real food. You can be assured that you are nurturing your microbiome, body, and mind with the highest-quality, anti-inflammatory nutritive.

There are five primary elements of life or building blocks of nature that make up everything we perceive through our senses – Space, Air, Fire, Water and Earth – that exist both within us and in the world around us. The three doshas are derived from the five elements. The five elements organize themselves into three essential principles of life: movement, metabolism, and structure, known in Sanskrit as vata, pitta, and kapha. These principles, which we can think of as air, fire, and earth, are the forces that govern every natural function and regulate every process within our mind and body. Since each of us is a unique expression of nature, we each have an inherent tendency toward one or more of these principles. This explains why we each responds so differently to the same stimulus. Some of us are naturally earthier, while others are more fiery or airy. As we discuss the functions and characteristics of each of these principles, notice which ones you most identify with. Each of the mind-body principles – vata, pitta, and kapha – have a balanced expression and an out-of-balance expression. When these principles are circulating in the mind-body physiology in appropriate proportions, we feel healthy and happy, and all our bodily functions work in harmony with one another. Unhealthy lifestyle choices can imbalance the doshas. However, when we follow an improper diet and make unhealthy lifestyle choices, these principles may become disturbed and cause distress in mind or body. Click on the link below for a video prepared for you about the importance of knowing the five elements, the characteristics of each of the three doshas and how you can align yourself with these energies.

https://bit.ly/30C7hz8

The six tastes of life and their primary elements: sweet, pungent, bitter, astringent, sour, and salty.

SWEET

- Proteins, carbohydrates, and fats. Most nutritive, builds tissue.
- Grains, dairy, starchy vegetables, fruits, bread, pasta, nuts, seeds, oils, sweeteners, eggs, and animal products
- Primary elements: Earth and Water
- Pungent:
- Essential oils
- Stimulates digestion and detoxification
- Peppers, ginger, radishes, onions, garlic, turmeric, cinnamon, cloves, and basil
- Primary elements: Fire and Air

BITTER

- Alkaloids, glycosides
- Anti-inflammatory and detoxifying
- Green and yellow vegetables, green leafy vegetables, rosemary
- Primary elements: Air and Space
- Astringent:
- Tannins, fiber
- Healing, compacting
- Beans, legumes, vegetables, apples, pomegranates, nuts, non-herbal teas
- Primary elements: Earth and Air

SOUR

- Organic acids
- Promotes appetite and digestion
- Citrus fruits, berries, tomatoes, yogurt, cheese, fermented foods, pickles, vinegar, alcohol
- Primary elements: Earth and Fire

SALTY

- Mineral salts
- Promotes digestion
- Salt, sea vegetables, fish, shellfish, animal products, soy sauce, condiments
- Primary elements: Fire and Water
- Proteins, carbohydrates, and fats
- Most nutritive, builds tissue
- Grains, dairy, starchy vegetables, fruits, bread, pasta, nuts, seeds, oils, sweeteners, eggs, animal products
- Primary elements: Earth and Water

According to the Ayurvedic philosophy, the universal life force manifests in three different energies, or doshas, known as Vata, Pitta, and Kapha. We are all made of a unique combination of these three life forces. As these life forces move into and out of balance, the doshas can affect our health, energy levels and general mood. Therefore, it is important to know what foods are best of each of these doshas and how can we create balance when they become imbalanced.

See below some food recommendations based on each dosha.

FOOD FOR THE DOSHAS

- Vata
- Favor: sweet, sour, salty
- Reduce: pungent, bitter, astringent
- Include warm, oily, heavy, and grounding foods to reduce dryness, digestive imbalances, and emaciation
- Decrease gas and bloating by cooking with aromatic herbs (cinnamon, cardamom, bay) and chew roasted fennel seeds after meals.
- The qualities of the vata include cold, light, dry, sharp, irregular, rough, mobile, quick, and changeable.

The characteristics of the Vata are thin, light frame; variable digestion and sleep patterns; dry skin and hair; cold hands and feet; quick movement and speech; quick and imaginative; resistant to routine; and welcoming to new experiences. When vata is balanced, it is energetic, creative, adaptable, proactive, good at communicating, spontaneous, enthusiastic, and lively. When vata is imbalanced, it shows an overactive mind, anxiety, worry, inconsistency, insomnia, constipation, gas, bloating, and fatigue. To balance your vata, minimize pungent, bitter, and astringent flavors and increase sweet, sour, and salty flavors.

FOOD FOR THE DOSHAS: PITTA

- Favor: sweet, bitter, astringent
- Reduce: pungent, sour, salty
- Include cool foods and liquids to reduce inflammation, heartburn, irritability, rashes
- Alleviate excess acidity by cooking with cooling herbs (cumin, coriander, fennel, cilantro)

Qualities of pitta include hot, light, oily, intense, penetrating, pungent, sharp, acidic, and moist. The characteristics of pitta are medium build, strong appetite, warm body temperature, sound sleeping for short periods, sharp intellect, direct and precise, organized routine, ambitious, and courageous. When pitta is balanced, she is bright, warm, friendly, focused, intelligent, decisive, good at naturally leader, good at digesting, and passionate. When pitta in imbalanced, she is angry, irritable, excessively critical, judgmental, and aggressive; and she gets skin rashes, Inflammation, and indigestion. To balance pitta, minimize sour, salty, and pungent flavors and increase sweet, bitter and astringent flavors.

FOOD FOR THE DOSHAS: KAPPA

- Favor: pungent, bitter, astringent
- Reduce: sweet, sour, salty
- Include light, dry, warm foods to reduce weight, congestion, allergies, fluid retention, and sluggishness. Kindle the digestion with some freshly sliced ginger before meals

Qualities of kapha include cold, heavy, solid, stable, smooth, oily, slow, steady, and soft. The characteristics of kapha are heavyset; smooth skin and thick hair; deep, sound sleep; slow moving; good stamina; easygoing; methodical; thoughtful; detail oriented; and accustomed to routine. When kapha is balanced, she is steady, consistent, loyal, strong, grounded, supportive, loving, content, calm, and patient. However, when kapha is imbalanced, she is dull, inert, needy, attached, congested, overweight, complacent, lethargic, overly protective, and resistant to healthy change. If you are feeling a little unmotivated, lethargic, and dull; or have put on some extra weight, have sluggish digestion, or can't get out of bed, there's a likelihood that this is an expression of excess kapha in your mind-body physiology. Therefore, it is time to balance your kapha by minimizing sweet, sour, and salty flavors and increase pungent, bitter, and astringent flavors in your food.

Using the Six Tastes to Balance the Doshas: Here are sample recipes that contains all the six tastes that you may find enjoyable. Also, see the dosha modifications for your dosha balance.

RECIPE: VEGETABLE BARLEY CASSEROLE

Ingredients

3 cups bite-size vegetables, such as carrots (sweet), zucchini (sweet, astringent), yellow squash (sweet, astringent), potatoes (sweet, astringent), and leeks (pungent, sweet), kale or other dark leafy greens (bitter)

- 1 tablespoon ghee (sweet)
- 3 cups cooked barley (sweet)
- 1 cup fresh or frozen corn (sweet, astringent)
- 12 cup fresh or frozen peas (astringent)
- ½ teaspoon turmeric (pungent, bitter, astringent)
- ½ teaspoon black pepper (pungent)
- 2 tablespoons thyme (pungent)
- 1 tablespoon oregano (astringent, pungent)
- 4 tablespoons Bragg's Liquid Aminos or tamari (astringent, salty)

- 3 tablespoons vegetable broth powder
- 1 cup tomato sauce (sweet, sour)
- 2 tablespoons arrowroot dissolved in ½ cup water, for thickening (sweet)
- Breadcrumbs, for topping (sweet)

Preheat the oven to 350 degrees (F). In a large skillet, sauté the bite-size vegetables in the ghee. Combine with the rest of the ingredients except the breadcrumbs. Pour into an oiled 9-by-12–inch casserole dish and sprinkle liberally with the breadcrumbs. Bake for about forty minutes or until bubbling. Serves ten people.

Dosha Modifications: By substituting some of the herbs and grains in this casserole, you can make this recipe more balancing for your dosha type.

Vata: Use cardamom, ginger, cumin, and/ or bay leaf instead of thyme and oregano. Use rice or a wheat-based grain instead of barley.

Pitta: Add cumin, coriander, and/ or fennel instead of thyme.

Kapha: Add more turmeric, chili pepper, or other pungent spices. Instead of potatoes, use more leafy greens, yellow squash, and zucchini.

RECIPE: A DELICIOUS GREEN SALAD

Ingredients

- 2 pounds washed and stemmed spinach (bitter, astringent)
- ¼ cup sliced radishes (pungent)
- ½ cup crumbled Gorgonzola cheese (sweet, sour)
- ½ cup dried cranberries or currants (sweet, sour, astringent)
- 1 cup honey-glazed walnuts, optional – recipe follows (sweet)
- Toss all ingredients together and arrange on plates.
- Honey-Glazed Walnuts, optional
- ½ teaspoon ghee (sweet)
- 1 cup walnut pieces (sweet)
- 1 tablespoon honey (sweet)

Heat the ghee in a skillet. Toss in the walnuts and sauté for two minutes or until golden.

Remove from heat. Add the honey and coat the walnuts well. Let cool completely before using.

Dosha Modifications: Adding a little bit of salt to the dressing adds in this taste to make the salad a six-taste meal. Here are a few ways to tailor this recipe with dressings to balance your dosha:

Vata: Choose a poppy seed dressing (sweet) or a salad dressing made with a base of olive oil or sesame oil.

Pitta: A sweet or astringent dressing made with olive oil will help pacify Pitta. Also, try adding avocado (sweet, astringent).

Kapha: Try a Dijon mustard dressing (pungent) or your favorite spicy salad dressing. Reduce or eliminate the Gorgonzola cheese and add half a cup of cooked garbanzo beans (astringent) instead.

Here are three nourishing herbal smoothies.

ASHWAGANDHA BANANA AND ALMOND BUTTER SMOOTHIE

Ingredients

- 1 banana, frozen
- 1 cup oat milk, unsweetened
- 1/4 cup raw almond butter
- 1 tablespoon Ashwagandha powder
- 1 teaspoon cinnamon powder
- A dash of honey (only if you'd like to add a hint of sweetness)

Directions: Place ingredients in a blender and blend until smooth. Serve immediately. Serves two.

CALMING CHERRY CHAMOMILE SMOOTHIE

Ingredients

- 1 cup coconut milk
- 1/2 cup cold chamomile tea
- 1 cup frozen cherries
- 1 cup frozen mangos
- 1 teaspoon flax seeds
- 1 tablespoon coconut oil
- A few drops of liquid stevia

Directions: Place ingredients in a blender and blend until smooth. Serve immediately. Serves two.

LAVENDER AND WILD BLUEBERRY SMOOTHIE

Ingredients

- 1 cup of frozen wild blueberries
- 1/2 banana
- 1/2 avocado
- 1/2 cup cold lavender tea
- 1 cup of your favorite plant-based milk of choice
- 1 teaspoon of pure vanilla extract
- A few drops of liquid stevia (optional)

- 1/2 cup of ice

Directions: Place ingredients in a blender and blend until smooth. Serve immediately. Serves two.

A BREAKFAST RICE CEREAL RECIPE

You can modify this recipe for your dosha by substituting other grains for the rice. See suggestions below.

Ingredients

- 1 cup basmati rice, (or other grain) uncooked* (sweet)
- 2 cups water
- ½ teaspoon salt, if desired (salty)
- ½ teaspoon nutmeg (pungent, bitter)
- 1 teaspoon cinnamon (pungent, sweet)
- ½ teaspoon clove (pungent, bitter)
- 1 cup vanilla soy milk (can substitute regular milk or other milk alternative) (sweet)
- ¼ cup blueberries (sweet, sour, astringent)
- 1 tablespoon maple syrup (or honey) (sweet)
- 1 teaspoon ghee (optional)

Combine rice, salt, and water. Bring to a boil, reduce heat, and simmer. Add soy milk and spices. Just before serving, add ghee, maple syrup, and blueberries on top. Serves two.

Optional: serve with sautéed fruit.

Dosha suggestions are as follows:

Kapha: Try apple or pear.

Vata: Add peaches or ripe banana.

Pitta: Instead, sprinkle some raisins or dates on top.

You can use cooked grains – just add soy milk and follow the rest of the directions.

Dosha-Balancing Grain Choices:

Vata: Rice, wheat, couscous, quinoa*, and buckwheat kasha*

Pitta: Wheat, rice, barley*, rolled/ whole, rolled/ groats

Kapha: Buckwheat kasha*, corn mush/ polenta, millet*, rye rolled/ groats, oats, barley rolled whole*

Increase water when cooking by ½ to 1 cup.

In summary, I have taught you how to balance your energy with nutritional foods and how to prepare balanced meals to increase your wellness with food that you enjoy. It is important to remember to eat a variety of colorful foods in order to receive a broad spectrum of basic nutrients, including proteins, water, fats, carbohydrates, minerals, and vitamins.

5

MOVEMENT

"Lack of activity destroys the good condition of every human being, while movement and methodical physical exercise save it and preserve it."

— PLATO

One of my favorite ways to create movement is through yoga. Research studies have shown that traditional yoga – the union of physical, mental, and spiritual practices that includes breathing exercises, asanas (body postures), chants, and meditation – can reduce stress and improve immunity and lung functions. While a consistent yoga practice often gets recognized for improving flexibility, many overlook its ability to improve muscular strength as well. Poses like the down dog and plank, along with all the warrior poses, build up muscle fibers to tone and strengthen your muscles. And while many forms of physical fitness emphasize muscle strength, yoga balances both strength and flexibility. Yoga is a practice that creates balance (both mind and body), so we must remember to incorporate both if we want to maintain a sustainable practice to last us a lifetime.

According to Dr. Deepak Chopra, when we are coping with emotional pain, a purely mental or intellectual approach usually is not enough. Although our minds may try to think their ways out of pain, they can quickly become confused or trapped in repetitive thought patterns that intensify our emotional turmoil. When we invite our bodies and spirits to be part of the healing process, however, transformation can unfold. The ancient wisdom tradition of yoga offers practices that unite the mind, body, and spirit, allowing us to experience deep emotional well-being and restful awareness. When your physical, intellectual, and spiritual selves are working in union, your life becomes more balanced, and you become more flexible, both physically and emotionally.

The Seven Spiritual Laws of Yoga program that Dr. Deepak Chopra and Dr. David Simon developed is rooted in India's ancient Vedic tradition. It is designed to raise your level of physical vitality, clear emotional blockages from your heart, and awaken your happiness and enthusiasm for life. The remarkable benefits of yoga, which include improved flexibility, balance, muscle tone, endurance, and vitality, only hint at the extraordinary power of this deeply spiritual practice. When adhered to and practiced mindfully, yoga can unlock your full creative potential, capacity for love and compassion, and ability to find success in all areas of your life. The Seven Spiritual Laws of Yoga brings spirituality back to yoga. It shows how the Seven Spiritual Laws play a crucial role in yoga's path to enlightenment while providing listeners with a wealth of meditation techniques, mantras, breathing exercises, and yoga poses. Whether a newcomer to yoga or an experienced practitioner, The Seven Spiritual Laws of Yoga is a portal to yoga's deeper spiritual dimension and a beautiful step to a happier, more harmonious, and more abundant life.

The remarkable benefits of yoga, which includes improved flexibility, balance, muscle tone, endurance, and vitality, only hint at the extraordinary power of this deeply spiritual practice. When adhered to and practiced mindfully, yoga can unlock your full creative potential, capacity for love and compassion, and ability to find success in all areas of your life. According to Dr. Deepak Chopra, the Seven Spiritual Laws of Yoga brings spirituality back to yoga. It shows how the Seven Spiritual Laws play a crucial role in yoga's path to enlightenment while providing listeners with a wealth of meditation techniques, mantras, breathing exercises, and yoga poses. Whether a newcomer to yoga or an experienced practitioner, The Seven Spiritual Laws of Yoga is a portal to yoga's deeper spiritual dimension and a beautiful step to a happier, more harmonious, and more abundant life.

The seven laws of Yoga are as follows:

1. The Law of Pure Potentiality: Your internal reference point is your soul rather than seeking constant approval by others.
2. The Law of Giving and Receiving: The universe operates through dynamic exchange. When the life force is flowing freely through your body and mind, you are in natural alignment with the generosity and receptivity of the universe.
3. The Law of Karma (Cause and Effect): Every action we take generates a force of energy that returns to us in kind – as we sow, so we reap.
4. The Law of Least Effort: Nature's intelligence functions with effortless ease. There is rhythm and balance in the natural world, and when you are in harmony with nature, you can activate the law of least effort to maximize your rewards.
5. The Law of Intention and Desire: This is based upon the recognition that at the quantum field there is nothing other than energy. This is the field of pure potentiality. Be clear about your intentions and desires into conscious awareness and surrender the

outcome to the universe. Understanding that at the quantum level field, there is nothing other than energy has required faith and my complete trust.

6. The Law of Detachment: To acquire something in this world, you have to relinquish your attachment to the outcome. Attachment is based on fear and insecurity. According to the principles of yoga, the only true security comes from your willingness to embrace the unknown. Whenever I have experienced challenges in my life, this law has served me well over the years because I was willing to embrace the unknown and relinquished the outcome.

7. The Law of Dharma: This states that every human being has a purpose in life. You are a unique person; you have unique abilities and your way of expressing them.

Every experience in the mind is accompanied by shifts in the body's chemistry. When you say, "I feel depressed," you are acknowledging that your body is generating disturbing sensations. These sensations result from changes in hormone levels and in the pattern of nerve firings within your nervous system. These physiological shifts can persist long after the emotionally upsetting experience that first triggered them. Over time, your mind-body system reflects your emotional history. Through yoga, you can release the emotional toxicity stored in the body. Just as changing thought patterns can influence the body, changing the position of the body can influence the mind and facilitate emotional release. As you stretch your muscles and expand your range of motion, you shift the bodily patterns that trap emotional pain. Yoga poses, breathing practices, and meditation release the constriction and free the flow of the vital life-force energy known as prana.

Let go of the need to compare yourself to others! If you think that nothing will work out, you can repeat to yourself, "Life is good. Life always leads me in the right direction." The universe is conspiring in your favor. The perfect solution is unfolding for you right now.

Instead of getting stuck in feelings of helplessness, affirm, "I always have choices and opportunities. My life is constantly improving. I see new possibilities in every moment."

Recognize your thoughts that are not serving you and let them go. Be patient with yourself and know that at first, you may not believe what you are telling yourself. Refuse to believe the dire messages your mind is generating; they are simply conditioned thought patterns that you have created. You have the power to create new, more nurturing beliefs. This takes time and effort, but the rewards are well worth it.

Slow, deep, conscious breathing is effective in promoting the relaxation response to counter elevated levels of stress hormones. An important component of yoga is paying close attention to what is always going on in the body and locating and releasing any areas of tension. Although you can feel the healing effects of yoga after just one session, regular practice is required if you want to experience the full benefits yoga offers. In addition, yoga should ideally be practiced with the guidance of an experienced teacher. There are many yoga styles and traditions to choose from. Some have a greater focus on physical fitness, while others are more meditative and spiritually based. It is important to explore and find a practice and teacher that resonate with you.

As we discussed in Chapter 4 about nutrition, diet may play a part in protecting against depression. Mediterranean countries have low rates of depression compared to countries farther to the north, and it is not just because they get more sunlight or have a more relaxed way of life. One large-scale study tracked almost 3,500 people living in London for five years and found that those who ate a Mediterranean diet were thirty percent less likely to develop depression. Researchers speculate that the foods in the Mediterranean diet may act synergistically to enhance mood. Olive oil, nuts, and fatty fish are rich in omega-3 and other unsaturated fatty acids that can help restore balance to the body. Fresh fruits and vegetables contain flavonoids and phytochemicals that are full of antioxidants and folates (B vitamins).

Depression is sometimes described as "anger turned inward." Many people were taught growing up that it is not polite to express anger and other emotions. They push their "unacceptable" feelings down for many years, but ultimately, these disowned feelings may manifest as depression. After my loving mother passed away unexpectedly, I was in great pain. I was suppressing my deep sadness and feeling of such an incredible loss in my life. I felt a sense of numbness and disconnection from myself and others. It was through the healing power of yoga movements and focused breathing that I learned to minimize and eventually wash away my incredible sadness and my deep sense of loss, and I was able to accept, acknowledge, and love myself again. Reestablishing this connection inside yourself is not difficult, but if you have developed a habit of avoiding yourself or your feelings, it will require some discipline and commitment to overcome the old patterns and establish new patterns. After my mother died unexpectedly, I found helpful to write my feelings in a journal at the beginning of the day. At the end of the day, I wrote about what I was grateful for in my life, and I poured it all out on the page with grace and gratitude for God's benevolence.

If you are experiencing depression or sadness, you may find journaling helpful, especially if you do it daily. Also, practice yoga or your favorite exercise daily and pay close attention to your breathing, your body language, your tone of voice, your muscle tension, and where your mind moves to distract you; notice everything you can with loving indifference. You are neither approving nor disapproving of your behavior and neither trying to change it nor keeping it the same. Maintain this gentle self-awareness of those behaviors that are walling you off from yourself. Without trying to change your habits, you will find that just by being fully present and aware, the grip of the old habits will fade, and new fresh and spontaneous responses will take their place. Listen and notice the new growth of what is starting to emerge in you. You will release a lot of physical and emotional tension at this point, so you will need channels to release it. I find that self-care is important for my wellbeing, and I enjoy yoga, swimming, massage, dancing, and singing.

Let your heart guide you to any music, movies, or natural surroundings that can also support your release process. Being a kapha, I like energizing music with a solid bassline accompanied by higher tones. I like all kinds of drums, bells, chimes, panpipes, and electric keyboards. If you are a vata, you are overactive; a peaceful and mellow mood using meditative music that has a soft and melodic tone, such as a cello, and a balance wind instrument, like a flute, will have a grounding and calming effect and will balance you. If you are a pitta, an excellent way to create balance would be listening to nature sounds, particularly music that incorporates running water and ocean waves. Also, music with mid-range tones featuring instruments like the saxophone or any type of slow and arrhythmic percussion or drum will have a soothing and balancing effect on a pitta dosha.

In summary, bringing yourself back into balance means that you are aware enough to make decisions and can put them into practice. Be patient with yourself, and do not expect any single practice or technique to completely end your sadness or depression. Be kind to yourself and remember that your essential nature is pure love, pure spirit, and pure potentiality.

THE ENERGY CODES

"You are Energy. Pure. Spirit Energy."

— DR. SUE MORTER

In her book, *The Energy Codes*, Dr. Sue Morter tells us that "It all begins with working with the energy patterns that form your experiences. That is because the root of emotional and physical challenges from stress at work to discord in relationships to chronic pain and financial lack, is energy. Or rather, these challenges are the result of subtle blockages within your body's energy field. And it is possible for you to remove subconscious and energetic blocks to your health, achievement, and manifestation." To help you do so, Dr. Sue Morter developed her world-renowned Energy Code teachings, so you can clear the way for profound healing and the ability to cocreate everything in your life.

Dr. Morter explains that everything that makes the entire universe is energy in varying wavelengths vibrating at different frequencies. The highest frequencies are purely ranging from non-visible to visible to the human eye. Sound frequencies are just more condensed versions of the same energy. Our thoughts and our emotions are merely different vibration frequencies, and even our physical form is nothing more than compressed energy. Our physical body is composed of an infinite number of different frequencies. The five main circulatory systems of the body are respiratory, hormonal, immune, cardiovascular, and digestive. Everything is connected, and we are part of the entire universe that is made of that same energy. We all can manage the energy flowing through our system. And to make it more unified – that is what the Energy Codes teach you how to do it. Our experiences affect our energy, which, in turn, creates our next experience, and through the feedback loop, we create our own reality. We are the creators of our lives. This gives us tremendous freedom and power. There is evidence that the physical universe is expanding. Our lives are parts of the universal creation, as is our consciousnesses. This means that we are constantly evolving. Each of these codes corresponds to a chakra, a major energy center in the body, from the base of your spine to the crown of your head.

Here is a brief overview of the *Energy Codes* as explained by Dr. Sue Morter.

1. The Anchoring Code: The root chakra is the first chakra. It is located at the base of the spine. The breathwork is the central channel breath. The body areas affected include the bone, skeletal structure, hips, legs, feet, genitals, the base of the spine, kidneys, body's life force, teeth, nails, blood, the building of cells, and adrenal glands. The channel breath helps us shift our focus from the external world to the energetic core (our true essence), self-mastery, and high physical energy. Some of the yoga poses for greater integration and balance are the chair, the warrior one, the pyramid, the tree, and the standing forward fold pose.

2. The Feeling Code: The sacral chakra is the second chakra. It is located just below the navel. The breathwork is the vessel breath. The body areas affected include the bladder, prostate, womb, pelvis, nervous system, lower back, fluid function, adrenal glands, and sex organs. The adrenal glands are also known as suprarenal glands; they are small, triangular shape glands located on top of both kidneys. They produce hormones that help regulate your metabolism, immune system, blood pressure, response to stress, and other essential functions. The vessel breath is the language of the soul. As we sense and feel the energy shifts taking place in our body, we begin the dialog between our true self –the soul and the mind. Some of the yoga poses for greater integration and balance are

the boat pose, pigeon, yogic bicycle, seated spinal twist, and breath of fire pose.

3. The Clearing Code: The solar plexus chakra is the third chakra. It is located three inches above the navel at the base of our sternum. The body areas affected include the digestive system, muscles, stomach, liver, diaphragm gall bladder, lower back, autonomic nervous system, spleen, and pancreas. The autonomic nervous system is a component of the peripheral nervous system that regulates involuntary physiologic processes, including heart rate, blood pressure, respiration, digestion, and sexual arousal. It contains the three anatomically distinct divisions of sympathetic, parasympathetic, and enteric. The solar plexus breath allows us to open the door to the subconscious to manifest our wishes. Some of the yoga poses for greater integration and balance include the camel pose, bow pose, reverse table pose, crescent warrior, and breath of fire.

4. The Heart Code: The heart chakra is the fourth chakra. It is in the center of the chest, beneath the breastbone. The breathwork is the heart coherence breath. The body areas affected are the heart, chest, circulation, arms, hands, lower lungs, rib cage, skin, upper back, and thymus gland. The thymus gland makes the white blood cells which are part of the immune system and help fight infection. Our immune system protects us from outside invaders, such as bacteria, viruses, fungi, and toxins. It is made up of

different organs, cells, and proteins that work together. The coherence breath is the vibrational frequency that we experience as love. This energy is the highest vibration that we can experience here in this physical form. The yoga poses for greater integration and balance include the triangle pose, the thread needle pose, the fish pose, and the reclined spinal twist.

5. The Breath Code: The throat chakra is the fifth chakra. It is the power of life itself. It is located halfway between the heart and the throat centrally at the base of the neck. The breathwork is the manifesting breath. The body areas affected include the mouth, throat, ears, neck, voice, lungs, chest, jaw, airways, back of the neck, arms, thyroid, and parathyroids glands. The thyroid gland plays a major role in the metabolism, growth, and development of the human body. The parathyroid glands are four small glands of the endocrine system that regulate the calcium in our bodies. The manifesting breath is the most powerful tool we have for manifesting energy in physical form. Remember that everything in this world is energy. The breath is energy, vitality, or life force. It is life itself. The yoga poses for greater integration and balance are the cobra, plow, bridge, and toning with sound (om, ma, ha).

6. The Chemistry Code: The third eye is the sixth chakra. It is located inward from the center of the forehead toward the middle of the brain, above and between the eyebrows. The breathwork is visionary

breadth. The body areas affected include the eyes, base of the skull, ears, nose, left eye, left brain, sinuses, pituitary gland, and pineal gland. The pineal gland is key to the body's internal clock because it regulates the daily circadian rhythms of the body, including signals to make the body feel tired, sleep, wake up, and feel alert around the same time each day. The pituitary gland is an important pea-sized organ. If your pituitary gland does not function properly, it affects vital parts like your brain, skin, energy, mood, reproductive organs, vision, growth, and more. It is the "master gland" because the hormones it produces regulate important functions, such as growth, blood pressure, and reproduction. This code gives us the key to shift our physiology from "threatened" to "safe." It teaches us how to create the optimal physical environment for increasing the presence of the soulful self. The yoga poses for greater integration and balance include the downward dog, shoulder stand, child's pose, exalted warrior, and balancing pose.

7. The Spirit Code: The crown chakra is the seventh chakra. It is located at the top of the head. The breathwork is the central channel breath. The body areas affected include the upper skull, skin, cerebral cortex, right eye, right brain, central nervous system, and pineal gland. The cerebral cortex is responsible for many higher brain functions such as sensation, perception, memory, association, thought, and voluntary physical activity. The cerebrum is the large, main part

of the brain and serves as the thought and control center. The central nervous system is made up of the brain and spinal cord. The central channel breath enables us to focus on quieting the thinking mind and becoming truly present so we can readily perceive the soulful communications that are constantly rising within our body and act according to them without hesitation or doubt. This is the creatorship and the soulful self. The yoga poses for greater integration and balance include the corpse, headstand, rabbit, and the wide-angle forward pose.

In summary, bringing yourself back into balance means that you are aware of the benefits of these energy codes and can put these energy codes into practice. Be patient and kind to yourself, and remember that your essential nature is pure love, pure spirit, and pure potentiality.

7

SLEEP

"Sleep is when our soul actually refreshes our body."

— DR. DEEPAK CHOPRA

I n this chapter, I will teach you how to enhance your wellness by learning more about how to deepen your sleep cycles and rejuvenate your body. A good night's sleep is critical for your health because our brains sort the important elements of the day from the unimportant and stores memories, allowing for more efficient long-term memory recall. Our body regulates hormones such as cortisol (to help manage stress), human growth hormone (to repair muscle tissue), insulin (to regulate blood glucose), and others. Cell turnover rids waste from your cells, leaving the immune system restored. Chronic sleep deprivation impairs attentiveness, coordination, and reaction time. It also increases the risk of obesity, high blood pressure, heart attacks, diabetes, and depression. And sleepiness is an all-too-common cause of accidents and fatalities in the workplace and on highways.

Making sleep a priority takes time and patience, just like any other health behavior change. Consider the following tips for better sleep, from setting a sleep schedule to including physical activity in your daily routine. Some of the factors that can interfere with a good night's sleep include work stress and family responsibilities to unexpected challenges, such as illnesses. While you might not be able to control the factors that interfere with your sleep, you can adopt habits that encourage better sleep.

1. Stick to a sleep schedule. Set aside no more than eight hours for sleep. The recommended amount of sleep for a healthy adult is seven to eight hours. Most people don't need more than eight hours in bed to achieve this goal. Go to bed and get up at the same time every day. Try to limit the difference in your sleep schedule on weeknights and weekends to no more than one hour. Being consistent reinforces your body's sleep-wake cycle. If you don't fall asleep within about twenty minutes, leave your bedroom and do something relaxing. Read or listen to soothing music. Go back to bed when you're tired.

2. Pay attention to what you eat and drink. Don't go to bed hungry or stuffed. It is important to avoid heavy or large meals within a couple of hours of bedtime.

Your discomfort might keep you up. Nicotine, caffeine, and alcohol deserve caution, too. The stimulating effects of nicotine and caffeine take hours to wear off and can wreak havoc on quality sleep. And even though alcohol might make you feel sleepy, it can disrupt sleep later in the night.

3. Create a restful environment. Create a room that's ideal for sleeping. Often, this means cool, dark, and quiet. Exposure to light might make it more challenging to fall asleep. Avoid prolonged use of light-emitting screens just before bedtime. Consider using room-darkening shades, earplugs, a fan, or other devices to create an environment that suits your needs. Doing calming activities before bedtime, such as taking a bath or using relaxation techniques, might promote better sleep.

4. Limit daytime naps. Long daytime naps can interfere with nighttime sleep. If you choose to nap, limit yourself to up to thirty minutes and avoid doing so late in the day. If you work nights, however, you might need to nap late in the day before work.

5. Include physical activity in your daily routine. Spending time walking outside every day might is helpful and it is a good exercise. Regular physical activity can promote better sleep. However, avoid being active too close to bedtime.

6. Manage worries. Try to resolve your worries or concerns before bedtime. I highly recommend journaling what's on your mind daily and then setting it

aside and dealing with those worries the following day.

7. Stress management might help. Start with the basics, such as getting organized, setting priorities, and delegating tasks. Meditation also can ease anxiety.

8. Aging can also affect the quality of your sleep. You may wake up more often and have a less consistent sleep pattern than you did when you were younger. One of the most common and pronounced sleep changes that comes with aging is waking up more frequently. The most likely cause is some type of physical discomfort, such as the need to use the bathroom or reposition an achy joint. Other changes that are part of normal aging, include getting less sleep overall and spending less time in the rapid eye movement (REM) cycle, the dream phase of sleep. These changes can vary quite a bit between individuals, and in general, they affect men more than women.

According to Dr. Hillip Hagen, you can try some simple techniques to limit disruptors and improve your quality of sleep. Some of these techniques include reviewing your medications and supplements with your doctor or pharmacist and consider changes to their use that could be affecting sleep quality. Stop drinking fluids within two hours of bedtime to minimize trips to the bathroom. If pain keeps you awake at night, talk to your doctor to see if taking over-the-counter pain medication before bed may help. While this may not stop you from waking up, you may have an easier time falling back to sleep.

If you snore loudly and feel tired even after a full night's sleep, you might have sleep apnea, a potentially serious sleep disorder in which breathing repeatedly stops and starts. I used to snore loudly, and my primary doctor recommended a polysomnography (a sleep study), a comprehensive test used to diagnose sleep disorders. Polysomnography records brain waves, the oxygen level in your blood, heart rate, and breathing, as well as eye and leg movements during the study. I did my polysomnography at a sleep disorders unit within a hospital, but it can also be done at a sleep center. In addition to helping diagnose sleep disorders, polysomnography may be used to help initiate or adjust your treatment plan if you've already been diagnosed with a sleep disorder. Polysomnography monitors your sleep stages and cycles to identify if or when your sleep patterns are disrupted and why. There are different types of home sleep apnea test devices using different combinations of sensors. They generally record your breathing rate and airflow, as well as oxygen levels and heart rate.

There are three main types of sleep apnea: obstructive sleep apnea, central sleep apnea, and complex sleep apnea. My polysomnography showed that I suffered from obstructive sleep apnea that occurs when the throat muscles relax. The throat muscles support the soft palate, the triangular piece of tissue hanging from the soft palate (uvula), the tonsils, the sidewalls of the throat, and the tongue. When the muscles relax, your airway narrows or closes as you breathe in. You can't get enough air, which can lower the oxygen level in your blood. Your brain senses your inability to breathe and briefly rouses you from sleep so that you can reopen your airway. This awakening is usually so brief that you don't remember it. You might snort, choke, or gasp. This pattern can repeat itself five to thirty times or more each hour all night, impairing your ability to reach the deep, restful phases of sleep. I now use, every night, a CPAP device that keeps obstructions from blocking my ability to breathe when I am asleep. The CPAP mask and tubing provide a gentle flow of pressurized, filtered air to keep my airway open, and I can enjoy a good night's sleep.

Central sleep apnea occurs when your brain doesn't send proper signals to the muscles that control breathing. This form of sleep apnea occurs when your brain fails to transmit signals to your breathing muscles. This means that you make no effort to breathe for a short period. You might awaken with shortness of breath or have a difficult time getting to sleep or staying asleep. Complex sleep apnea syndrome, also known as treatment-emergent central sleep apnea, occurs when someone has both obstructive sleep apnea and central sleep apnea. If you think you might have sleep apnea, see your doctor. Treatment can ease your symptoms and might help prevent heart problems and other complications.

Some medical research suggests that intermittent fasting can also improve your sleep. Intermittent fasting means that you don't eat for a period each day or week. Some popular approaches to intermittent fasting include alternate day fasting. Eat a normal diet one day and either completely fast or have one small meal (less than 500 calories) the next day. Eat a normal diet five days a week and fast two days a week. Eat normally but only within an eight-hour window each day. For example, skip breakfast but eat lunch around noon and dinner by 8:00 p.m. Intermittent fasting improves your health. Losing weight and being physically active help lower your risk of obesity-related diseases, such as diabetes, sleep apnea, and some types of cancer. For these diseases, intermittent fasting seems to be about as beneficial as any other type of diet that reduces overall calories.

According an Intermittent-fasting article published in the Beacon Health System, Intermittent fasting is safe for many people, but it's not for everyone. Skipping meals may not be the best way to manage your weight if you're pregnant or breastfeeding. If you have kidney stones, gastroesophageal reflux, diabetes, or other medical problems, talk with your doctor before starting intermittent fasting.

According to Dr. Eric Olson, lack of sleep can affect your immune system. Studies show that people who don't get quality sleep or enough sleep are more likely to get sick after being exposed to a virus, such as a common cold virus. Lack of sleep can also affect how fast you recover if you do get sick. During sleep, your immune system releases proteins called cytokines, some of which help promote sleep. Certain cytokines need to increase when you have an infection or inflammation or when you're under stress. Sleep deprivation may decrease the production of these protective cytokines. In addition, infection-fighting antibodies and cells are reduced during periods when you don't get enough sleep. Using technology late at night can keep you from getting a good night's sleep, whether you're doing work on your laptop or scrolling through social media posts on your smartphone. Some scientific research has even shown that the light from your phone might suppress your body's production of melatonin, the hormone that regulates your sleep cycle.

Our bodies need sleep to fight infectious diseases. Long-term lack of sleep also increases your risk of obesity, diabetes, and heart and blood vessel (cardiovascular) disease. Being well-rested is important to your health, mood, and productivity. Dr. Deepak Chopra recommends everyone get eight hours of sleep each night. Dr. Chopra recommends practicing mindful breathing before bedtime. The best way to do this is to count to four as you breathe in and then count to six as you breathe out. "This slows your breathing from an average of fourteen [breaths] to an average of eight [breaths] per minute." Mindful breathing restores self-regulation and calms the mind. Dr. Chopra recommends another breathing exercise that he says you can use to fall asleep, and it revolves around a popular mantra – words you repeat while breathing to help you relax. Say "so" as you inhale and then say the word "hum" as you exhale. The "so hum" mantra is derived from Sanskrit and often used in yoga and other forms of meditation. Much like mindful breathing, this meditative mantra is meant to help calm your mind. A 2015 study published in The Journal of the American Medical Association found that "mindfulness meditation" practices helped improve sleep quality for subjects who were experiencing insomnia symptoms. Another way to relax when you're trying to fall asleep is to close your eyes just before you lay down and recap the events of your day in your mind. On the screen of your consciousness, you see yourself as if you were on a video screen, "Observe the day, without judging it, and then let it go." When you do that, you actually let go of all the stresses that happen during that day, and you go to bed with a fresh start for the next day."

In this chapter, I have taught you how to enhance your wellness by learning more about how to deepen your sleep cycles and regenerate your body. I hope you will incorporate some of these practices to your daily evening routine to enable you to enjoy a restful sleep on a regular basis.

8

MEDITATION

"To make the right choices in life, you have to get in touch with your soul. To do this, you need to experience solitude, which most people are afraid of because in the silence you hear the truth and know the solutions."

— DR. DEEPAK CHOPRA

In this chapter, I will teach you, and you will experience, the journey from activity to silence. Meditation is a practice to train and focus your attention and awareness. It is an opportunity to destress the mind. Current scientific research validates that having a regular meditation practice produces tangible benefits for mental and physical health, including improved immune function, reduced worry, anxiety, and depression, increased rejuvenation, anti-aging hormones, better cognitive skills, more meaningful relationships, and enlightenment. Meditation can even change gene expression to promote healing, self-regulation, and balance.

What is stress? Stress is a state of mental or emotional strain or tension resulting from adverse or very demanding circumstances. It results from perceiving obstacles to the fulfillment of our needs and desires. Through the "fight/ flight/ freeze" response, your body responds to these perceived obstacles or threats. What stresses are you experiencing right now? How do they make you feel? Fight, flight, freeze. In response to stress, the heart beats faster/ pumps blood more quickly and blood pressure rises. You consume more oxygen and expel more carbon dioxide. perspiration increases. The adrenal glands pump out adrenaline, noradrenaline, and cortisol. The immune system becomes suppressed, and the blood platelets become stickier. In a fight response, a pitta dosha defends against threats and respond to a threat by fighting and exhibiting irritability. A vata dosha responds to a threat by fleeing; a vata dosha tends to avoid the thereat and becoming anxious and fearful. A kapha dosha defends herself by freezing, numbing, detaching, and giving up easily.

During meditation, the body shifts into a state of restful awareness, which counterbalances the fight/ flight/ freeze response. Therefore, the heart rate slows/ pumps blood more slowly, blood pressure normalizes, perspiration decreases, adrenal glands produce less adrenaline and cortisol, immune function improves, breathing slows down, and platelet function normalizes. According to Gabriel Roger, chief meditation officer at the Chopra Institute, you can practice meditation anywhere, and it is best practiced in a comfortable seated position with your eyes closed. Use pillows and blankets if needed. Avoid lying down unless you are unable to sit upright comfortably, and minimize potential distractions, such as phones, music, and television. When meditating, you can chant a mantra, which is thought with no meaning. Most thoughts have a sound and a meaning. Meaning holds the mind at the active thinking level. When thinking a mantra, there is nothing to hold the mind at the active thinking level. "So Hum" is a mantra meditation using the vibration of the breath. The best way to meditate is sitting comfortably with your eyes closed. Gently introduce the silent repetition of the mantra, "So Hum." On the inhale, mentally repeat the word, "So." On the exhale, mentally repeat the word, "Hum." When you become aware you have drifted away to other thoughts, sounds, or sensations, gently return your attention to your breath and the repetition of "So Hum."

You can end your meditation by letting go of the mantra. Remain with your eyes closed for a few minutes; then, gently move back into activity. Use a watch or meditation app to time your meditations and always allow for the proper time to come out of meditation, even if it means ending meditation early. You can have several different experiences during meditation, including thinking thoughts and restlessness, falling asleep, and accessing silence. It is best to avoid seeking a particular experience or result during meditation; instead, approach meditation with innocence and non-judgment. Each meditation is unique and will be best suited for you at that moment. Practice effortlessness and allow the natural process to unfold.

When you are meditating and your mind is wandering, simply return to the mantra. Thoughts are a normal part of meditation and usually indicate some release of stress, which is a good thing. Thoughts outside of meditation are generally memories or desires, taking us into the future or the past. To break the pattern of repeated thinking about the same thing, take a few deep breaths and bring your awareness to the breath. Your breath can only be in the present moment, so awareness of it brings you out of thoughts of the future or past. Then, think of something that you like or something that brings you joy. Your thoughts are creating your reality all the time. We project our fears, doubts, joys, and sorrows on the world all the time. By changing your thoughts and your attitude, you can change your world. Buddha said, "Our life is shaped by our mind, we become what we think. Suffering follows an evil thought; joy follows a pure thought."

There will always be thoughts, but the quality of the thoughts will change. As we progress with our spiritual practices, we become more of a witness to our thoughts rather than identifying with the thoughts themselves. Eckhart Tolle said, "You are the sky, everything else are just clouds." Instead of struggling against thoughts or getting attached to them, notice them, and allow them to drift in and out, like clouds on a summer's day.

The definition of worrying is "praying for what you don't want," which is why worrying is one of the most destructive things we do to ourselves. Think back to this time last year. What were you worried about then. Did it happen? Even if it did, I assume you survived. As the philosopher Michel de Montaigne said," My life has been full of terrible misfortunes – most of which have never happened." Nothing in life should be feared; it only needs to be understood. However, while you are doing that, use your breath. Our breath is probably our most under-utilized tool. It is always with us and always available. Worrying and negative expectations take you into the future. Your breath is always in the present. Whenever those worrying thoughts arise, move your awareness to your breath. Take a few deep breaths and just observe the breath for a couple of minutes. Allow the breath to center and ground you. Worrying also depletes your energy, whereas the breath is energizing. Keep in mind the following four intentions in your daily meditation: joyful, energetic body; loving and compassionate heart; reflective, alert mind; and lightness of being. These can be repeated silently at the end of your meditation practice or before sleeping at night. They are to enliven health, harmony, and happiness on all levels of life. You can intend them for yourself or also include others with them.

As a Chopra Certified Health Instructor, I practice a mantra meditation technique called primordial sound meditation, which assigns a mantra based upon your date and place of birth. According to the theory that underlines primordial sound meditation, the universe expresses a different vibration frequency at different times during the day. You can appreciate this principle by considering how the environment feels at dawn from the way it does at high noon or at dusk. This primordial sound or mantra is said to represent the sound of the cosmos. This primordial sound can be used as a meditation vehicle to take you back through the doorway from individuality to universality which is the goal of meditation.

My favorite meditation involves intoning mantras aloud to create a healing resonance in the mind and body. There are mantras associated with each of the seven energy centers in the body, known as chakras. The chakras are major junction points between consciousness and the body, and each one is associated with a specific vibration. Envisioned by the ancient seers as wheels or vortices of life force, they sometimes have been associated with major neural networks or hormonal systems. Each center identifies a core human need. When the center is open, the energy that flows through the chakra allows you to meet those needs more effortlessly.

The chakra meditation is an amazing experience. You receive nourishment from the earth in the first chakra, and creative juices flow from the second chakra. Your intentions are empowered in the third, and your heart is open and exchanging love with those around you in the fourth chakra. You are spontaneously expressing your higher self in the fifth, and you are in touch with your inner voice in the sixth chakra. Then, energy moves into the crown chakra, and you remember your essential nature as infinite and pure love. You know yourself as a spiritual being temporarily in a human body and mind. To experience this meditation, sit comfortably with your spine upright, close your eyes, and visualize the site of the energy center you want to focus on. Take a deep breath, and on inhalation, chant the mantra in one long syllable. Feel the sensation in your body and notice the sense of alert calm in your mind after each mantra. Envision energy flowing effortlessly from the base of the spine through the different energy centers and rising to the top of your head. Notice how you feel in the meditation and how it affects you when you return to your active life.

The first chakra is the root chakra, known in Sanskrit as muladhara. It is in the base of the spine, and it governs your most basic survival needs. When energy is flowing freely through this center, you have confidence that you can meet your core needs without struggle. When there is a blockage in this area, you will tend to experience anxiety and worry. The law of karma governs this first energy center. On the physical plane, every action you perform results in a corresponding reaction. This first chakra, which connects you with the earth, provides essential information as to the potential nourishment or toxicity that is available to you because of the action you are taking. The color of this chakra is red, and it is associated with the element of earth and the sense of smell. The mantra for this first chakra in "lam."

The second chakra, called svadhisthana, is associated with creativity in all its expression. It is located in the area of the sexual organs, and the energy of this center can be used for biological reproduction. The law of least effort is lively in the second chakra. When the vital energy is flowing through your center of creativity, you cocreate your life. When you are aligned with your creative juices, the expressions that emerge arise effortlessly. The second chakra utilizes the raw material of the root chakra to create the world anew each day. The color for the second energy center is orange. It is associated with the element of water and the sense of taste. The mantra for the second chakra is "vam."

The third chakra, manipura, is in your solar plexus. It is the seat of your power in the world. When the center is open and flowing, you can translate your intentions and desires into manifestation. When it is blocked, you feel frustrated and ineffectual. The seeds of intentions and desires reside in your soul. The process of manifesting your desires is first to bring them into consciousness, then expand your awareness through meditation, then release your intentions and detach from the outcome. The color of the third chakra is yellow like the sun. It is associated with the element of fire and the sense of sight. The mantra to clear and enliven the third chakra is "ram."

The fourth chakra represents the unifying energy of love and compassion. Known as anahata, the heart chakra is dedicated to overcoming separation and division. When the heart center is blocked, there is a sense of alienation from others. When the heart center is open and flowing, you feel connected at a deep level with all beings in your life. The law of giving and receiving governs the heart chakra. Every act of giving is simultaneously an act of receiving. Each time you welcome a gift into your life you are providing an opportunity for someone to give. The color of the fourth chakra is green. It is associated with the element of air and the sense of touch. The mantra that awakens the fourth chakra is "yum."

The fifth chakra is the throat chakra, called vishudda in Sanskrit, and it is the center of expression. When it is open and flowing, you have the confidence that you are capable of communicating your needs. When the fifth chakra is obstructed, a person will often feel that she is not being heard. The law of detachment governs the throat chakra. An open fifth chakra will enable you to express your truth without concern for sensors. The color of this chakra is blue. It is associated with elements of ether or space and the sense of hearing. The mantra to open the fifth chakra is "hum."

The sixth energy center is sometimes known as the third eye. Located in the forehead, ajna, as it is known in Sanskrit, is the center of insight and intuition. When this center is open, you have a deep sense of connection to your inner voice and feel guided in your choices. When it is blocked, there is a sense of self-doubt and distrust. The opening of this chakra is usually associated with a clear sense of connection with one's dharma or purpose in life. The law of dharma or purpose in life governs the sixth chakra. The color of the sixth chakra is indigo. It is associated with extrasensory perceptual abilities such as clairvoyance. The sense is inner sound, independent outside vibrations. The mantra to awaken the sixth chakra is "sham."

The seventh chakra, the consciousness chakra, known as sahawara, is visualized as a lotus flower at the crown of the lead. When the lotus unfolds its petals, the memory of wholeness is restored. You remember that your essential nature is unbounded and that your spirit is in disguise as a person. This is the full expression of yoga – the unification of being with action, of universality with individuality. The law of pure potentiality governs the seventh chakra. The color of the seventh chakra is violet. It is associated with the sense of compassion that comes from recognizing it as a reflection of yourself. The mantra to nurture the seventh chakra is "aum."

Every meditation technique offers something of value to the mind and body. A simple, effective, and easily learned mediation technique uses the breath along with a breathing mantra to quiet the mind and to relax the body. An easy meditation is known as the "so hum" meditation. To experience this meditation, sit comfortably where you will not be disturbed and close your eyes. For a few minutes, simply observe the inflow and outflow of your breath. Now, take a slow, deep breath through your nose while thinking the word "so." Exhale slowly through your nose while thinking the word "hum." Allow your breathing to flow easily, silently repeating "so hum" with each inflow and outflow of your breath. Whenever your attention drifts to thoughts in your mind, sounds in your environment, or sensations in your body, gently return to your breath, silently repeating, "So hum." Continue this process for fifteen to twenty minutes with an attitude of effortlessness and simplicity. When the time is up, sit with your eyes closed for a couple of minutes before resuming your daily activity.

In summary, I have taught you the benefits of various breathing and meditation techniques to reduce your stress and enhance your wellness. Every meditation technique offers something of value to the mind and body. A simple, effective, and easily learned mediation technique uses the breath along with a breathing mantra to quiet your mind and to relax your body. Enjoy!

YOUR EMOTIONS

"The best and most beautiful things in the world cannot be seen or even touched. They must be felt with the heart."

— HELEN KELLER

Ayurveda recognizes that your emotional balance is one of the fundamental pillars of health. Health is not merely the absence of disease; it is a state of physical, emotional, mental, and spiritual wellbeing. Ayurveda teaches that many physical ailments have an emotional root cause. Your bodymind is affected by your emotions and cultivating emotional freedom begins with awareness – awareness of your feelings, what you need, what you need to release, and what brings you joy and happiness. You all share a desire to be happy. You are conditioned to derive happiness from temporary, external sources.

When you identify yourselves and your happiness with objects outside yourselves, this is known as object referral. The opposite of object referral is self-referral – you identify with your inner self and internal state of well-being that does not depend on external circumstances. True joy is an internal state of awareness that allows you to be happy for no reason and is independent of circumstances, events, people, and things in your lives.

Your essential nature is pure, unbound consciousness with infinite possibilities

When you perceive your physical and psychological needs are met, you feel comfort, pleasure, happiness, contentment, satisfaction, and cheerfulness. Your fundamental human needs are attention, affection, acceptance and appreciation. Emotions are derived from your perception of needs being met or not met. You feel emotions as sensations in your bodies that are associated with thoughts in your minds. You experience emotions in two ways:

- Comfort encompasses all the feelings that move you from constriction to expansion, including joy, peace, love, pleasure, delight, and gratitude.
- Discomfort includes all the feelings that constrict you, including distress, frustration, anger, regret, fear, pain, and sadness.

Secondary emotions are based on unmet needs that are not resolved and often lead to anxiety, hostility, guilt, and depression. Feelings not fully experienced can accumulate as emotional toxins (emotional ama). You can either react to unmet needs, which is an instinctual, conditioned, and learned behavior; or you can respond, which implies being aware and having a choice. All the doshas can experience every kind of emotion, though each dosha reacts to unmet needs in different ways.

The vata doshas react with feelings of anxiety, fear, worry, and guilt. They are likely to blame themselves and say, "what did I do wrong?"

The pitta doshas tend to feel angry or hostile. They are prone to blame others and say, "What did you do wrong?"

The kapha doshas tend to become sad and discouraged. They may ignore situations and withdraw and say, "I don't want to deal with it."

OUR SEVEN BIOLOGICAL RESPONSES

1. Fight-Flight-Freeze: The most primitive response grounded in the survival instinct, serving to keep the body protected based on fear and the perception that your environment is threatening acute stress.

2. Reactive Ego Responses: Psychological the equivalent of fight-flight-freeze attempts to control the environment through reactivity. Emotions are in the

domain of the ego, and when you perceive that needs not met, uncomfortable feelings are generated, and you react to them. You naturally defend against threats, and when you respond to a threat by fighting, you exhibit irritability, loss of temper, and defensiveness. This response corresponds to the pitta dosha. When you respond to a threat by fleeing, you tend to avoid the threat, become anxious, and become fearful. This response corresponds to the vata dosha. Sometimes, when perceiving a threat, you defend yourself by freezing, numbing, detachment, and giving up easily. This response corresponds to the kapha dosha.

3. Restful Awareness Response: Your body relaxes, and you bypass the reactive response internal reference shifts from ego to spirit, witness the activity of the mind, and become capable of conscious choice-making. This is best cultivated through the practice of meditation. Your heart rate, blood pleasure, respiration, perspiration, stress hormones, platelet stickiness go down our anti-agent hormones go up.

4. Intuitive Response: Being aware of your interpretations choosing conscious observation and authentic expression present moment awareness in your daily lives facilitates conscious communication and restful awareness (meditation) plays a key role.

5. Creative Response: Applying a new context or meaning to a situation or circumstance solutions emerge by quieting down inner dialogue. There are seven steps for awakening the creative response: inten-

tion, information gathering and analysis, incubation, insight, inspiration, implementation, and integration.

6. Visionary Response: Living from the collective soul vision of what is possible ability to access collective dreams and the archetypal realm consciously participates in the story of your lives. Some of the questions for awakening the visionary response include, "What stories would you like to enact? Who inspires you? What attributes do you connect with?"

7. Sacred Response: Sense of self expands beyond constricted ego; unity consciousness compassion is a natural expression transcend, "What's in it for me?" and dwell in, "How can I be of service?" As a wave is to the ocean, each of us is to spirit. Based on the work of Marshall Rosenberg (Nonviolent Communication: A Language of Life), use this process to gain clarity about how you feel, identify what you need, and take responsibility to consciously communicate your needs to another person: What happened? State the facts. What are you feeling? Describe how you feel, choosing words that describe only the emotion, and avoid victimization words. What do you need that you are not receiving? Identify the need you have that is not being met. What are you asking for? Make your request with a level of respect, rather than a demand. What is the gift or opportunity in this situation? Observe what you benefited from the practice of this process.

When your needs are being met, you feel bright, carefree, delightful, enthusiastic, glowing, hopeful, invigorated, joyful, loving, optimistic, peaceful, quiet, radiant, secure, thankful, warm, upbeat, and vivacious. When your needs are not being met, you feel afraid, anxious, bitter, confused, embarrassed, frightened, frustrated, guilty, helpless, irritable, invisible, jealous, lonely, overwhelmed, pessimistic, resentful, unhappy, and withdrawn. Words are powerful; therefore, avoid words that encourage victimization, such as abandoned, betrayed, cheated, diminished, manipulated, neglected, pressured, unappreciated and unwanted. Here are the steps to emotional clearing: take responsibility for what you are feeling, identify your emotion, witness the feeling in your body, express your emotion in private to yourself, release your emotion through a ritual, share your emotion with a good listener, and rejuvenate with a celebration.

Pranayama practices activate the body's parasympathetic nervous system, which governs the rest-and-digest response, also known as the relaxation response: slow, rhythmic belly breathing, complete breath, nadi shodhana, ujjayi, and bhastrika.

Nadi shodhana is an "alternate nostril breathing" and is a simple yet powerful technique that settles the mind, body, and emotions. You can use it to quiet your mind before beginning a meditation practice, and it is particularly helpful to ease racing thoughts if you are experiencing anxiety, stress, or having trouble falling asleep.

Ujjayi breathing is a technique that allows you to

calm your mind by focusing on your breath. This helps you override thoughts that could possibly distract you from your meditative state. Used in the practice of yoga, it also creates a sound that assists you in synchronizing your movements with your breath.

Bhastrika pranayama is the process of rapid inhalation and exhalation which gives a boost to the body and, hence, is aptly called the yogic breath of fire. So, the next time you feel like your body needs energy, try bhastrika pranayama.

Journaling is also highly recommended for emotional release Set intentions for what you would like to release. Develop a vision statement for your life. Describe in detail the sights, sounds, feelings, and experiences you would like to see unfold in your life.

What would you like to see in these areas of your life: physical body and health, spiritual, family; career/ business, friends and loved ones, material possessions. The grandest vision that I would like to share with you encompasses twelve areas of my life.

A few years ago, I participated in the Lifebook workshop taught by Jon and Missy Butcher. Through their teachings, I learned to deep focus and clarify twelve areas of my life. Lifebook takes you far deeper, right down to the core of who you are, how you show up in the world, and how you perceive reality. I learned not only how to strengthen each of these twelve dimensions, but I also explored the vital and often surprising interplays between each one. To create a vision for your life, I highly recommend that you also, create a comprehensive plan that not only includes financial wellbeing, but it covers all the important areas of your life including the following twelve areas.

HEALTH AND FITNESS

You must define exactly what you want, why you want it, and what you need to do to get it. While it is impossible to avoid all stress in life, minimizing stressors, and managing the way you respond to stress can have important benefits. This can include taking a break from the situation, listening to calming music, and progressive relaxation. Even taking a deep breath can help. Exercise is known to be beneficial for reducing stress and the long-term effects of stress on your health. This includes doing something active during a stressful situation and exercising regularly to improve the way your body responds to stress. While all forms of exercise seem to work, much research and practice have focused on specific types of exercise including yoga and tai chi. The most important thing is to make exercise part of your day, especially now. Other effective strategies traditionally include meditation and relaxation exercises. Research shows that getting enough sleep is also critical for reducing stress and the impact it has on your health. Eating a healthy diet can reduce the effects of stress as well. In summary, a healthy lifestyle includes stress management as well as a nutritional diet and regular activity.

Intellectual wellness is the ability to be open to new ideas, critical thinking, and learning new skills to create the potential for sharing with others and use it for the betterment of the community. Intellectual wellness promotes creative mental stimulation as well as learning new and exciting things. A good way to increase your intellectual wellness is to read for fun. Reading, especially something you enjoy, can improve your intellect by stretching your mind to think about things you normally don't think about. Improve your skills for studying and learning. Also, learning new things about the way your mind processes information can be a vital tool to helping you succeed. Write down your thoughts or journal frequently. Taking the time to write down thoughts or journal frequently can help those who struggle with expressing their feelings or in general for anyone who is trying to make sense of what they are feeling inside. Being able to identify your feelings and understanding yourself more and your actions increase intellectual wellness by exposing your mind to deeper thinking. You hold the power to move you quickly and forcefully toward your life's goals.

EMOTIONAL

It is important to explore the nature of your emotions and discover how you can further develop your emotional intelligence. Make your emotions work for you, instead of living in reaction mode. Feel free to share your feelings and thoughts with your family and close friends. Emotional intelligence refers to our ability to understand and effectively use our different emotions. It's not so much about controlling your emotions, which implies that you restrain, suppress, or deny them; rather, it's about managing your emotions, which involves being flexible with your thinking, behavior, and responses and being opened to stay with feelings both pleasant and unpleasant. We can learn and practice emotional intelligence skills at any age or stage of life. And we should: emotional intelligence is linked to better mental and physical health and overall life satisfaction.

CHARACTER

This is the foundational category that affects every other area of your life. During this profound exploration, you'll define the person you need to become to achieve the life you desire, living emotionally, and financially successful and holistic lifestyle. You'll learn how to consciously choose the character traits you want to build into your life and develop a strategy for accomplishing them. A person's character is who they are. We all think about a lot of things that are not godly, and things we would be ashamed of if they were available for all to know. Abraham Lincoln once said,

"Character is like a tree and reputation like its shadow. The shadow is what we think of it; the tree is the real thing." My reputation is what others think of me, which may or may not be true, but my character is who I am. Your character is the real you in the sense that you cannot separate what you do from who you are.

SPIRITUAL

According to Dr. Deepak Chopra, "Everyday life is impossible without holding your own set of beliefs." Just because belief exists silently doesn't make it less powerful. Most people are guided by a belief in the work they do, their religion, their loyalty to their family, and all kinds of values they hold dear. During this journey into your spirituality, you'll examine, define, and document your deepest beliefs about life, the world, and your place in it. You'll discover a strength deep within and gain a valuable new perspective on the purpose and meaning of your life.

Love Relationships: You'll achieve clarity on what you want in this area of your life and identify what steps you can take to create and nurture an extraordinary love relationship. What would your ideal love relationship look like? Is trust is one of the most important factors in a relationship? If you don't trust the person you are with, then it is probably not a healthy, stable relationship and you most likely feel insecure about it. How about respect? No amount of love is worth giving up who you are and the respect you deserve. Love is not a justification for disrespect or abuse. Partners must be respectful of each other and who they are for a healthy relationship to grow. How about communication? Communication is key in any relationship to define boundaries. You need it to express feelings, needs, and expectations. You need it to solve conflicts and you even need it when it comes to intimacy. Without good communication, how can anything in the relationship be clear and the rest of these values be strengthened? You will define the values and expectations for your love life.

PARENTING

This is a profound exploration for parents and non-parents alike. This category is important because the future of the whole human race depends on at least some of us doing it right. You will have to decide what kind of parent you would want to be. According to psychologists who study parenting, there are four main styles of parenting: autocratic, authoritative, permissive, and unengaged. The styles differ in terms of how much involvement you have in your child's life and how much control you try to exert over your child's behavior. Being a good parent means you need to teach your child the morals of what is right and what is wrong. Setting limits and being consistent are the keys to good discipline. Be kind and firm when enforcing those rules. Focus on the reason behind the child's behavior. Being a parent myself, I know that some of the most important parenting qualities are loving and being flexible with your child, being open-minded, and being easy-going. Being flexible doesn't mean you let your child get away with murder. Find the balance between accommodating and dominating; your child will reward you with greater respect and self-restraint. It's said that children absorb ten percent of what you say and ninety percent of what you do. Modeling lives and breathes in your behavior: your words, actions, and feelings (spoken and unspoken) are deposited into your child and shape his or her core identity. Whether you like it or not, kids develop values and a life philosophy based on their parents' choices.

Also, it is important to empower your child, nurture independence, fostering responsibility, and encouraging self-reliance. Likewise, children need consistent schedules and routines. Healthy structure, limits, and boundaries lay the foundation for good habits that last a lifetime. They also nourish confidence by reducing fears and anxieties in children. Often, things such as your health or the health of your marriage are kept on the back burner when a child is born. If you don't pay attention to them, they will become bigger problems down the road. Take good care of yourself physically and mentally. Take time to strengthen your relationship with your spouse. If these two areas fail, your child will suffer, too.

SOCIAL

Here, you will thoughtfully evaluate your relationships with friends and extended family. You'll come to understand which relationships contribute positively to your life and which ones drain you. You will learn what actions you can take to strengthen your most important relationships and what you can do to let unhealthy relationships go. Why is social behavior important? From a psychological point of view, social behavior helps to promote our emotional well-being. Social behavior is desirable because it means that people will cooperate and systems can run effectively. You must behave according to the standards of the culture in which you are living at any given time. There are specific types of greetings and rituals that convey respect. There are little things that you must avoid doing in certain cultures or you will be frowned upon or, worse, literally arrested, confined, deported, or worse still.

CAREER/ BUSINESS

Explore the meaning and rewards of a great career/ business. Learn strategies to take any career/business to a higher level – and make more money in the process. Proactivity is required for career/ business success. First, it is a mindset. You need to realize that no one cares more about your career/ business and its financial impact than you do. You need to be proactive if you want career/ business advancement. Make things happen that the company needs to have happened, manage the process, and as a result, you will get paid more and be more successful. Being proactive and do more than expected and do not assume that your stakeholders are aware of how you are over-performing. That is why you need to regularly remind your stakeholders through performance reviews, regular reports, one-on-one meetings, and team meetings. The truth is that both performance (over-delivering) and being likable are important. Keep in mind to treat people like they want to be treated. It is also important to develop your skills. It is a fact of life that having certain skills can significantly increase your earning ability. You can develop a high level of competence with a unique combination of valuable skills. This collection of abilities makes you unique, valuable, and prosperous.

FINANCIAL

This is an important category, and you need to deeply explore the true nature of money – what it means to you, what it is, where it comes from, and how wealth is created and achieved. From this process of self-discovery, you will come to view yourself and your financial life and enable you to create your financial plan to enable you to achieve financial freedom, leading you to a better quality of life-based on your life vision.

QUALITY OF LIFE

In this category, you will identify how you wish to spend the hours, the days, and the years of your life. You will discover how it can lead to rewarding spiritual, intellectual, and emotional breakthroughs and improve who you are as a human being. Quality of life is an overarching term for the quality of the various domains in human life. It is an expected standard that consists of the expectations of an individual or society for a good life. These expectations are guided by the values, goals, and socio-cultural context in which an individual life. The quality of life is a subjective, multi-dimensional concept that defines a standard level for emotional, physical, material, and social wellbeing. It serves as a reference against which an individual or society can measure the different domains of a life.

LIFE VISION

You have thought through your entire life one category at a time. Now, you are going to experience the life you intend to create. For instance, if you're facing a financial challenge, you might sometimes find that the solution lies not in focusing directly on money or your career but on your intellectual life, or even your life vision. If you have a vision for your life, you will always know what areas of life to focus on at any given time and how to create extraordinary success in each of them without sacrifice or compromise. When creating your grandest vision, your emotional and intellectual ability holds the power to move you quickly and forcefully toward your desired life's goals.

In summary, your life vision and your desired quality of life will become clear when you examine your heart and when your actions are in alignment with your values. "Who looks outside, dreams, who looks inside, awakes." Keep the words of late mythologist Joseph Campbell in mind and follow your bliss. It is important to create your life vision, practice the steps for emotional clearing, and create a regular journaling practice to measure and celebrate the progress made in all the important areas of your life.

SELF-CARE

"Talk to yourself like you would to someone you love."

— BRENÉ BROWN

In this chapter, I will teach you how to establish a daily routine and tend to your needs for lasting health and happiness. Self-care is important practice in achieving a healthy and holistic lifestyle. What exactly is self-care, and how do you do it?

In her article published in the Harvard Business Review, author Amy Jen Su shares a few ideas.

Self-care. At the heart of self-care is your relationship and connection to yourself. As part of your job, it means that you understand what you need to be your most constructive, effective, and authentic self.

Make self-care an important part of your day-to-day work. Weave it naturally into the course of your workday.

Become aware when you are not taking care of yourself and engage in self-compassion, avoid self-neglect, and plan for self-care management.

Surround yourself with people that are supportive. Meaningful relationships are a critical part of self-care.

At the heart of self-care is your relationship and connection to self; therefore, rather than defining self-care narrowly as just physical health, you need to pay attention to a wider set of criteria, including care of the mind, emotions, relationships, environment, time, and resources. Rather than having self-care be something "outside" of work, it's important to weave it naturally into the course of your workday. To do so, make peace with your inner critic and cut yourself a break. Recharge throughout the week – make sure you're getting enough sleep and time with the people who boost your mood. Protect your thinking time, celebrate small successes as they occur, and learn to notice when you have started slipping out of self-care mode.

In the previous chapter, I shared with you a few ideas about how to resolve unresolved emotions, practice emotional clearing, and how Ayurveda recognizes that emotional balance is one of the fundamental pillars of health. Over the years, I have learned to focus and clarify important areas of my life, including body, mind, and soul. To self-care my body, I like to practice restorative yoga, go for walks, and remember to drink six to eight glasses of water per day. If you are working, take time to stand up at your desk and maybe even walk away from your desk and do some stretches depending on time availability. I highly recommend that you take time to self-care your mind by listening to a motivational podcast, reading a few pages of a book that you like, meditating, getting out for a walk, doing some deep breathing, and just letting your mind wander and enjoy the moment. Last but not least, to self-care for your soul, journal daily and write down three things you're grateful for, listen to a couple of songs that inspire you, make plans to have fun with a friend, make yourself a cup of tea and put your feet up and sip slowly, tell your family and friends how much you love and appreciate them, and watch a crazy video on YouTube that makes you laugh. The time of day that you practice self-care for each of these areas may vary according to your schedule but make sure that you include these self-care practices in your daily activities. You deserve daily self-care to be and feel at your best.

It is also important to engage in self-reflection. Our values and worldviews can directly affect our self-care, especially in the areas that include our ability to feel gratitude, our place in the natural world, and our acceptance of ourselves and others. Many people find solace and comfort in their deeper values, beliefs, and practices. The following questions are provided to help you reflect on several ways to view the world that may affect your self-care practice.

1. Do you tend to wake up every morning with a sense of gratitude or drag yourself out of bed bracing for a trouble-filled day?

2. Do you typically count your blessing throughout the day, or do you use valuable time to ruminate on problems and conflicts?

3. Do you tend to work on connecting to and supporting others, or do you often find yourself acting as an outsider or competitor?

4. Do you tend to sing your colleagues' praises, or do you put energy into gossiping about those around you?

5. Do you typically strive to consciously banish hard feelings, or do you often harbor and focus on resentments?

Create a self-care plan. Stress can be managed by direct and indirect coping strategies. Direct approaches include removing the stressor, recognizing, reframing, and changing your perception of the situation so that it is no longer stressful, removing yourself from the source of stress, or limiting your exposure to the stressor. Indirect methods involve finding ways to minimize the impact of stressful situations. They include exercising, healthy eating and sleeping habits, relaxing, meditating, setting aside time for yourself, working with others to solve problems, asking for help, and counseling. Your goal is to choose and incorporate a daily and/or weekly self-care practice that works for you. Decide that self-care is important and make a commitment to it. Share your plan with a friend or family member. Make it a weekly practice to review and share your progress with your designated self-care support person.

In order to establish a daily routine and tend to your needs for lasting health and happiness, I will also share with you a four-step plan for resilient living written by Amit Sood, MD. The first step is to train your attention. Life's happiest moments and lasting memories need an immersive experience. With deeper attention and delayed interpretations, we can enjoy the immersive experience and lasting memories. Seize your memorable moments before they depart unappreciated. Make each moment count.

The second step to cultivating emotional resilience includes gratitude, compassion, acceptance, meaning, forgiveness, and relationships. Together these timeless principles provide the foundation for emotional resilience. One good way to experience gratitude could be to send silent gratitude to three to five people daily.

Compassion is the practice of the golden rule. With compassion, you recognize that all of us struggle, are fighting little or big battles, and deserve each other's kindness. Being compassionate to yourself is the beginning of your journey toward having compassion for the world. Self-compassion is humble integration of your imperfections into your view of the self, with an eye toward growth and improvement. Your self-compassion is essential to your self-care and to your sustained happiness.

Acceptance has three components: acceptance of others, acceptance of yourself, and acceptance of situations. We can accept others and ourselves once we realize that all of us as humans have elements of imperfection and are fallible. We seek timeless wisdom and perfect love but are works in progress. We live with countless unknowns. Who created our universe and why? How long will you live? You can either allow yourself to be upset by these uncertainties or invite the wisdom of acceptance. Meaning, understanding meaning. Some important questions that we all have asked at one point, or another include Who am I? Why am I here? What is this world/ universe? Imagine you have to write an essay about yourself. What would you write? The specifics about who you are and what you do are the means; service and love are the meaning.

Love and meaning transcend age, race, gender, country, religion, and even our universe. Unlike all the other organs in our body, our minds have no natural system for getting rid of waste. Hurts pile up in our life but there is one cure that can dissolve all hurts for good: forgiveness, a voluntary choice, choosing the higher path, and leading a more thoughtful life driven by your principles.

Anger, holding grudges, and hostility can all lead to anxiety, depression, and irritability. By forgiving, you can enjoy improved health save energy, and have better relationships. Enjoying deeper and lasting connections within your community is one of your highest priorities and the final key to emotional resilience. Shared purpose is the thread that binds together the fabric of relationships. Acquaintances become lasting relationships when you have common goals.

The third step is creating a mind-body practice since a relaxed mind is a humble mind that is not struggling with fear, greed, or selfishness. Such a mind is happy. Some ideas to relax include deep breathing, yoga, reading, exercising, listening to music, meditating, playing with children, et cetera.

The fourth step is picking healthy habits and fun ideas that may help you decrease your stress and increase the energy available to you each day. You have a limited amount of physical, mental, emotional, and spiritual energy; therefore, it is important to choose only those challenges that are worthy of your time base on their relevance and ability to have an impact on them. We often take life more seriously than we need to; humor brings you into intentional presence. Find ways to insert humor into your life.

In summary, in this chapter, I taught you how to establish a daily routine and tend to your needs for lasting health and happiness. I believe that by implementing these ideas to your life, you have taken the important steps toward experiencing health, self-care, and sustainable happiness.

SPIRITUALITY

"Just like a sunbeam cannot separate itself from the sun, and a wave can't separate itself from the ocean, we can't separate ourselves from one another. We are all part of a vast sea of love, one indivisible divine mind."

— MARIANNE WILLIAMSON

In this chapter, I will teach you about spirituality. What is spirituality? Spirituality is defined as the quality of being concerned with the human spirit or soul as opposed to material or physical things. Spirituality is a personal experience; it is the feeling of oneness with the ever-expanding universe consciousness. It offers a sense of belonging and knowing your place in the universe. True spirituality leads to a sense of inner peace. Spirituality is the doorway to connecting with the divine. It is knowing what I am, who I am, and why I am here on this beautiful planet in this vast universe.

What do you believe? What deeply held beliefs are shaping your life? Are your beliefs empowering? Do they move you at a deep level, or are they holding you back? I believe that we are all part of one vibrational energy. Our consciousness is mysterious, deep, invisible, and eternal, and it connects everything and everyone everywhere. Spirituality is my way to connect with that something. Spirituality entails the feeling of oneness. I believe in oneness, wholeness, and unconditional love. And becoming all, we are human beings. Religions and myths contain truth and depict that truth with different words and metaphors. My thoughts and actions can affect an immeasurable number of people and events. Being kind and thoughtful to others is what it means to be human. Spirituality is about what I do, the choices I make, what I think, and how I spend my time.

What is your vision for spirituality? A simple life. A calm life. A steady life. A mission-driven life. A legacy life. A life of love. How do you want to feel in this area of your life? What do you want to be doing on a consistent basis? The spiritual path is a quest for self-actualization and a commitment to helping others achieve the same. One way we can all contribute is to take better care of our planet. No act is too small in making sure its natural beauty stays intact.

Our spirituality releases us from guilt, fear of death,

and fear of this life. What is your spiritual purpose, and what motivates you to achieve your vision? Is your purpose to create the highest possible quality of life for yourself and your loved ones and to help others around you do the same? Are you part of the shift from judgment to acceptance and from intolerance to embracing differences? How will you bring your vision into reality? Ask yourself what kind of positive habits, attitudes, and action steps you can implement. Some spiritual practices include forgiveness, meditation, spending time in nature, gifting, self-acceptance, et cetera. Will you pray and/ or meditate every day? It is how I commune with God, the source of creation, to replenish and heal my soul. It is important to connect with kindred spirits, surround yourself with like-minded people, and recognize the divinity within each of us.

If you want to experience God's love, I highly recommend the book *A Course in Miracles*, written by Drs. Helen Schucman and Bill Thetford, authorized for publication by the Foundation for Inner Peace in 1975. The teachings are designed to undo the illusion that you are separate in any way from God or your fellow humans. When we learn to live this truth consistently, fear, anger, and guilt give way to a profound sense of inner peace. *A Course in Miracles* systematically leads you to experience God's love in all your relationships through the practice of forgiveness, the willingness to receive and follow higher guidance, and the cultivation of miracle-mindedness. Happiness, peace, joy, and love are the natural outcomes of the book's teaching. Another inspirational book to have by your bedside is entitled *Year of Miracles*, written by one of my life coaches, Marianne Williamson. It is a collection of 365 spiritual readings, including prayers, meditations, declarations, and affirmations – one for each day of the year – that offers guidance, support, and enlightenment to focus your thinking. With this thoughtful meditative devotional, you can stay mindful and hopeful every day producing miracles in your life.

You are here for a reason, and the more you can connect to your purpose on the planet, the more you can live in the miracle one each day. According to Marci Shimoff and Dr. Sue Morter, there are three keys to discovering and living your passions and purpose: You each have two primary purposes for being on this planet. The first one is your universal purpose to expand your capacity to love and recognize that your true nature is love. This is the path of awakening to your divine essence. Your universal purpose is not about what you are specifically doing on the planet. It is about bringing presence and aliveness in the moment to everything you are doing. Your second purpose is your individual purpose, which is also known as your dharma or calling. Dharma is a Sanskrit word that is literally defined as "that which upholds." When you live your dharma, you are not only upholding your life, but you are also blessing all of creation. Ancient Vedic texts say that "when everyone is living their dharma, the world will have entered a golden age."

Your dharma is something you bring sacredness and devotion to and make a priority in your life. There are two ways to know what your dharma is. One is that it is what you are passionate about what you look forward to doing. The second is to recognize your natural gifts, talents, and inclinations. By cultivating and expressing your gifts and passions, you are aligning with your dharma. Do not compare your purpose to that of others. It does not matter if someone has already done something like what you feel inspired to do. Your purpose is here to be done by you. To clarify your purpose, look into your heart and get honest with yourself. What moves you and what sings to your soul? Answer the question, "What makes me come alive?" and do some of that each day. Here are some tools that can help you gain clarity about what your gifts are and what you love: The Passion Test (www.ThePassionTest.com) and Strengths Finder (www.gallup.com/cliftonstrengths).

According to Dr. Morter, passion and fear are the same energy. Fear is energy that is squelched, compressed, and contracted in your solar plexus. The result is having uncomfortable feelings of anxiety, tension, and nervousness. Passion is energy that is allowed to move through your body, and it can then be expressed out into the world. Your mind has a direct relationship with your solar plexus. If your purpose is not clear to you, you may have a blockage at the solar plexus level that causes imagined obstacles and fears projected into the future. By doing purposeful breathing exercises, energy can flow and then manifest into higher states of realization of your potential in the world.

Even if other people do not see what is possible for you, do not let that stop you. Live in the land of all possibilities, and know that if you have the vision, it is because it is possible for you. Living passionately in the land of all possibilities takes persistence. Your job is not to know the "how" but to know the "what." Stay in the present moment and take one step at a time, and the next steps will continue to reveal themselves. Take at least one measurable baby step toward your dreams every day. When you start taking a step toward living your passion every day, the universe will know that you are committed, and the entire providence will help you accomplish your life purpose.

In summary, through prayer and meditation, you can know your purpose and dharma more clearly. It also helps to visualize the fulfillment of your vision every day. Living in the miracle zone is being able to see what is possible.

OBSTACLES

"Every time you are tempted to react in the same old way, ask if you want to be a prisoner of the past or a pioneer of the future."

— DEEPAK CHOPRA

We've all made healthy resolutions or set goals with the best of intentions only to see them fall short or break down completely over time. Living a healthy and holistic lifestyle is an excellent goal to aim for, and the sooner you start the process, the healthier and happier you will be. Research and medical studies often promote the mental and physical benefits of a healthy lifestyle, so why do we still break our health and self-care promises when we know staying healthy helps us live a happier life?

Some of the obstacles that you may face include not having the right frame of mind and finding excuses for not committing to taking care of health on a daily basis. A popular reason why you may give up your healthy behaviors is because staying healthy could be complicated. Whether a life-long goal or a temporary objective, staying motivated requires commitment, complex planning, and follow-through. Therefore, establishing permanent healthy behaviors takes a different mindset and should not be undervalued. Part of your daily routine is to be aware of your eating and working environment. You will face constant pressures from a multibillion-dollar marketing industry that bombards you with quick, cheap, and tempting food options. No matter the medium, these highly targeted psychological messages leave you wondering if you are in charge of your eating behaviors or, instead, simply being conditioned.

Studies show that you overestimate how difficult exercise is. Often, you think physical exercise will be much worse than it ends up being. As a result, you tend to give up before you even begin. I know that if you are still reading this book, it is because you are committed to changing your lifestyle, and I want to help you stay motivated to accomplish your health and holistic lifestyle. Therefore, here are a few ideas to help you stay motivated. I will start by asking you a simple question: what will it take for you to make your healthy habits permanent? Being committed to the outcome is a good start followed by daily practice of your morning and evening routines and other healthy practices shared with you throughout this book. Anticipate some lapses, but you must establish a quick recovery and reward. We know the importance of our emotional state of mind; therefore, practice daily positive self-talk and create changes that are easy to continue over time. Your thoughts determine how you feel about yourself, which, in turn, affects your behavior, mood, interactions with others, and progress toward your goals. When you identify positive thoughts, make sure to practice them. Consider using the following path to help motivate your healthy behaviors. To get you started, list the behaviors you feel are unhealthy and develop positive and realistic goals for yourself. Identify why you want to meet this goal. What have you tried before? For instance, if you do not like lifting weights, try yoga or swimming. Select one of your identified behaviors you would like to change. Find multiple ways to remind yourself of your goal. Above all, stay motivated by visualizing a successful outcome.

The best way to overcome your obstacles is to create an action plan. For instance, every time you do not want to make time to exercise or want to eat junk food, brainstorm ways to change this behavior. Ask yourself this question: what will it cost you if you continue to have an unhealthy lifestyle? If you do not like the answer, devise a reward plan to promote a healthy living strategy, and identify in advance potential obstacles that could interfere with your goal. It is also important to set a date for when you want to achieve your goal and surround yourself with people that will support you and encourage healthy choices. You will experience minor lapses at some point during the journey. It's important to remember that a lapse is normal and doesn't always lead to a relapse. Relapse occurs when lapses string together and a person returns to his or her former state. Anticipate that a lapse can and will happen. Then, try and figure out what your trigger or triggers are for lapses. Some of the common triggers that may cause a lapse to include well-meaning people in your life: the time of day, your emotions, or a challenging life event. Dr. Chopra's quote at the beginning of this chapter comes to mind: "Every time you are tempted to react in the same old way, ask if you want to be a prisoner of the past or a pioneer of the future."

In summary, remember that you will face some obstacles when planning and implementing a stress-free environment and healthy lifestyle. I have taught you that you when facing obstacles, you replace destructive thoughts with more constructive ones. When you reach the goal date, evaluate, and reward your success. I know that if you are committed, committed to a healthy lifestyle, you will reach your goal.

CONCLUSION

"Happiness is when what you think, what you say, and what you do are in harmony."

— MAHATMA GANDHI

At the beginning of this book, I wrote about the need to create a healthy and holistic lifestyle. Therefore, throughout the book, I shared ideas to create a stress-free life in alignment with your values. Remember that a stress-free person lets go of judgment; is more accepting of others; appreciates how other people feel; tries to help in difficult situations; acts as a sympathetic listener; renounces anger and aggression; and works to maintain a harmonious, peaceful atmosphere at home and at work. As for longevity, a stress-free lifestyle is beneficial because it provides a buffer against stress. A recent study conducted on a large population (more than 800 samples) led at the University at Buffalo found that stress was linked to higher mortality rates, but not among those who helped others. It's in our nature to be sympathetic and kind to others while doing great good to ourselves at the same time.

In Chapter 1, I told you the story of one of my best clients, Michael who told me that he was too busy for self-care. I am happy to let you know that Michael has redefined his entrepreneurial success and he is now living a healthy and holistic lifestyle. He has adopted morning, noon, and evening routines and has implemented many of the body, mind, and spirit practices suggested thought this book. Now, he is living a healthy and holistic lifestyle. I hope that after reading this book, you, too, will know how to create a healthy and holistic lifestyle and feel excited about it because you now have a clear vision and you are no longer worried about an unhealthy lifestyle due to irresponsible choices or lack of commitment to a healthy lifestyle. In Chapter 2, I shared with how I solved my stressful life by creating a morning and evening routine. In Chapter 3, you learned the process of creating a healthy and stress-free lifestyle by creating healthy morning and evening routines that works for you. In Chapter 4, I taught you about nutrition and dove deeper into how to prepare balanced meals and increase wellness with food. In Chapter 5, I showed you how to create movement through yoga. In Chapter

6, I taught you about the important of knowing about your chakras and work with energy patterns that form your experiences. In Chapter 7, I taught you to enhance your wellness by learning about the importance of your sleeping cycles and how best to regenerate your body and mind. In Chapter 8, you learned the techniques to reduce stress and enhance wellness. In Chapter 9, I showed you how best to manage any unresolved emotions and practice emotional clearing. In Chapter 10, we established a daily self-care routine for lasting health and happiness. In Chapter 11, I taught you about spirituality. In Chapter 12, I showed you how to identify and how best to overcome obstacles. In Chapter 13, I assured you that you, too, can enjoy a stress-free, healthy, and harmonious lifestyle.

In summary, remember that living in the moment is one of the most important values of a holistic lifestyle. Our earthly body is a temple, and you should always take care of it. You must learn to tap into the hidden powers of your body and use them to your advantage. Meditation helps you relax and feel connected with the rest of the world. Because in the end, we are all connected. At the heart of self-care is your relationship and connection to self; therefore, rather than defining self-care narrowly as just physical health, you need to pay attention to a wider set of criteria, including care of the mind, emotions, relationships, environment, time, and resources. Rather than having self-care be something "outside" of work, it's important to weave it naturally into the course of your workday. To do so, make peace with your inner critic and recharge throughout the week. Make sure you're getting enough sleep and time with the people who boost your mood. Protect your thinking time and celebrate small successes as they occur. It is my heartfelt desire for you that you live a healthy and holistic lifestyle for many happy years.

ACKNOWLEDGMENTS

I was inspired to write this book because I have seen too many family business owners build a very successful business at the cost of their own health and neglected family relationships. Building a successful business takes time, courage, commitment, and money. It is not easy, but it is most important to take care of your own health. At the heart of self-care is your relationship and connection to self. Your earthly body is a temple, if you take care of your body-mind, it will serve you well.

I would like to thank my growing family! Stephen, my husband for over forty years, and our sons Michael and Tommy and their families, who are my biggest fans – always have been and always will be. I love and appreciate them deeply! My brothers Francisco, Sergio, Ruben, and Eloy and my sister Zulema are my proudest fans – seeing them beam with pride over my accomplishments and having their encouraging thoughts mean a lot to me. Thank you for your patience and for your unconditional love. Thank you for your sense of humor, your gentleness, and acceptance. May our family legacy make us proud!

Maria L. Ellis, MBA is a best-selling author of *Achieve Financial Freedom*, a roadmap to financial success. She is graduate of the Harvard Business School Owner-President Management Program and earned her bachelor's degree in business administration as well as her MBA from the University of Massachusetts in Amherst. As a former international banker, investments and real estate advisor, Maria has specialized in converting clients' financial objectives into successful action plans. Maria has both the know-how and the market contacts having worked at Bank of America, Citibank, the MONY Group, Northwestern Mutual, Citi Habitats, and Keller Williams New York City and Keller Williams Palm Beaches.

Maria's background includes board and leadership positions at the College of Mount Saint Vincent, the American Association of University Women, Harvard Club, New York City, Virginia Gildersleeve International Fund, and The Empire State New York City, AAUW. Maria is also a pro-bono consultant at the Harvard Business School Club of New York City Community Partners and applies her business skills to a variety of topics including strategic planning, marketing, finance, governance, and organizational development.

LET'S START A MOVEMENT WITH YOUR MESSAGE

In a market where hundreds of thousands of books are published every year and are never heard from again, The Author Incubator is different. Not only do all Difference Press books reach Amazon bestseller status, but all of our authors are actively changing lives and making a difference.

Since launching in 2013, we've served over 500 authors who came to us with an idea for a book and were able to write it and get it self-published in less than six months. In addition, more than 100 of those books were picked up by traditional publishers and are now available in bookstores. We do this by selecting the highest quality and highest potential applicants for our future programs.

Our program doesn't only teach you how to write a book – our team of coaches, developmental editors, copy editors, art directors, and marketing experts incubate you from having a book idea to being a published, best-selling author, ensuring that the book you create can actually make a difference in the world. Then we give you the training you need to use your book to make the difference in the world, or to create a business out of serving your readers.

ARE YOU READY TO MAKE A DIFFERENCE?

You've seen other people make a difference with a book. Now it's your turn. If you are ready to stop watching and start taking massive action, go to http://theauthorincubator.com/apply/.

"Yes, I'm ready."

OTHER BOOKS BY DIFFERENCE PRESS

Finish What You Start: Breaking out of the "Busy Mind, Restless Body" Trap to Create a Life You Love Even with ADHD by Meggie Houle

Weight-Loss Hypnosis: What to Do When Counting Calories and Carbs Isn't Cutting It by Pamela J. Leno

El Emprendedor Intrépido: Supere la Mentalidad Corporativa y Comience el Negocio de Sus Sueños by Clarisa Romero